Max Giovagnoli

TRANSMEDIA STORYTELLING

Imagery, Shapes and Techniques

Translated by Feny Montesano and Piero Vaglioni.
Translation edited by Dani Belko and Brandon Perdue

Cover Design: Alessandro Alpago (www.inventoridimondi.com)

ACKNOWLEDGEMENT

To Christy Dena and Nicoletta Jacobacci, Drew Davidson and Jeff Gomez, Henry Jenkins, Derrick De Kerkhove, Lance Weiler and Stephen Reinghold and all the other researchers and international producers who have helped and supported me over the years through their studies and experiences. Seven years after my first book about "cross media" narratives was released, the first book published in Europe that discussed this topic, my research now goes across the ocean and from the web *back to paper*. I knew it would be a long journey, full of work and practice. However, thanks to you, it has been an extraordinary experience too, full of voices and energy, adventures and meetings, strategies and new techniques in order to cross languages and learn how to tell our stories *differently*, around a new "digital" campfire.

To all my students,

and Characters

CONTENTS

PROLOGUE

For some time, there have been two definitions that pair the entertainment and information with communication worlds: *cross-media and transmedia*, both used to identify narratives that simultaneously develop on multiple media. As always, the difference lies in the nature of stories and in the way we choose to tell them. In this sense, there are:

- *narrative forms that don't change* when they are diffused on multiple platforms (for instance, a short film released in the same version at the cinema and, at the same time, on the web or during a TV show);
- *narrative forms* that share the same elements (plots, characters, atmospheres...) but *that change* depending on the publishing platform through which they are released (for instance, the same short film might be developed as a series or as a movie for the theater; its protagonist for a comic book series, etc...).

This latter way of storytelling, which is much more powerful and effective, is often identified as *cross-media* in some countries (for instance in Europe) still today. In others, particularly after the term has been accredited in the Hollywood film industry, it is known as *transmedia*. Finally, there are some countries (but it is just a small minority) in which a difference even exists between the term 'cross-media' (which is used for the stories that are exactly the same but on different media) and the term 'transmedia' (the stories that change depending on the distributive platform).

However, as often happens, in this case the academic definitions have been quickly exceeded by professional practice, and today, in the entertainment, information and communication industries, both terms – cross-media and transmedia – are used almost interchangeably, though with a certain preference for the second term. This is the reason why the 'transmedia' term has also been adopted as the title of this book and for the selection of the international cases of 'new narratives' in its pages. There are examples of stories created by major film studios and famous broadcasters, and by small independent companies, by powerful corporations, and *from below* by lively communities of users who have artistic or promotional aims. All of them are characterized by magic narrative universes that are too large in scope to be exhausted by a traditional *ballad-singer*.

INTRODUCTION

Before taking the field

Scene 1. The Brooklyn Bridge is 5989 feet long; that is to say, a little more than a mile. Everyday it is crossed by about 125,000 cars. Yet, from an exclusive point, after walking for half its distance, looking east, amongst the spires and the parallelepipeds of Downtown Manhattan, you can catch sight of it: Sixth Avenue, the *Avenue of the Americas*. The avenue that harbors skyscrapers, one after another, the Fox and CNN towers, NBC studios and the bright towers of Time Warner. In a word, the television industry that makes the shows, the news and the popular fiction series of today. And looking back, or rather below, where the bridge spans the opposite side of the Hudson River, there is a little park crossed by a path and some unplastered benches. This is the Brooklyn Height Promenade, exactly the point where all the famous directors place their cameras to create the collective imagination of the "Big Apple" and the "America Today" of the contemporary cinema. It's like a good omen: the cinema perspective under the bridge near the imagery and the content that flows like a river of our fantasies made real. Television is on the shore of the river in order to raise towers on towers, season by season, until you are not able to distinguish them one from another anymore... Until one night, while you are there standing on the bridge, suddenly your cell phone's vibration mysteriously brings you to your senses: is it just the usual promotional MMS from an unknown number? On the contrary: the sender is *Dexter!* He appears in the photo with a strange knife in one hand as he shares an address with you so that you can help him in his new "leather work", if you don't want to have dreadful trouble!

Scene 2. Spiderman and the Green Goblin face each other atop of one of the two double lancet windows of the Brooklyn Bridge: the former swings while hanging on his webbing and the latter flies around him threateningly, missing him with his *glider* missiles. The graphics and visual effects are perfect. Only a very trained eye could distinguish at first sight if it is a movie or a videogame. The narrative is captivating; the interface is invisible; soon the audience is drawn into the tale until the image is suddenly blocked and...to continue the tale, the audience finds out *something must be done.* But... what? Some research and you easily discover that the answer is in a comic book on sale at news-stands and comic shops: use your smartphone to capture the QR code printed on the comic's cover and you will soon get some advice about how to continue your online tale or, even, influence it while it develops!

Scene 3. Have you ever noticed that when Mickey Mouse turns his head, his ears don't change perspective, but stay still, one standing up more than the other on the back of his neck? Everybody always misses it in the comics, and even watching *Fantasia* on a cinema-sized screen few people would notice it. But if you tell this to Warren Spector, the inventor of *Epic Mickey,* the videogame that is linked to the most popular Disney icon in the world, he will tell you how many days he had to spend programming so as not to let the ears of Mickey Mouse move when the player was playing this *platform game...* So, this is more than comics! *But...what I am getting at?*

Telling stories which are distributed on multiple media is like creating a new geography of the tale and it requires the author and the audience to agree on some fixed and safe spaces for sharing, even if they can be altered to different combinations. Hence, before going on, it is important to clarify in this short introduction what the publishing and technological restrictions are, that are shared by all the different tales explained in these pages. The four cardinal points of "doing transmedia" are:

1. *Doing transmedia* means to involve multiple media in a publishing project, keeping the features and the language of each one, even if they are part of a single system of integrated communication;
2. *Doing transmedia* means to make the project's contents available on different technological platforms, without causing any overlaps or interferences, while managing the story experienced by different audiences;
3. *Doing transmedia* means to allow the multiple media to tell different stories but all exploring a common theme, even if it is experienced through multiple narrative perspectives;
4. *Doing transmedia* means to agree to give a part of the authorship and responsibility of the tale to the audience and other storytellers in order to create a participatory and synergistic story in the experiences of the different audiences of the tale.

Thus, exploring the narrative universe of a story by using transmedia is even more like a question of experience than use, and it makes compromises and challenges necessary for both the authors and the audiences. It is the proper founding act for the tale, and an excellent opportunity to influence the *homo ludens* of today who are longing for new and more active roles in the process of fantasy and imagery-making.

CHAPTER ONE

Think Transmedia

Media is like pollen, all around us, and inside of us. Each day we collect and stack up pieces from the media, reconstructing layer by layer their *invisible scripts,* and then we bring them to bed with us every night in our cement beehives. We are in contact with hundreds of communicative environments for 24 hours a day, we put up with about 3000 advertisements and by now we are accustomed to getting information and feelings from the media with the total confidence and the same fictional agreement of the five senses that nature gave us. But it is not always like this. The confluence of media involves everything in our collective imagery-making, and by now it enables us to love and engage with a complexity, rather than a simplicity in our stories[1]. And at the same time it brings information and messages to us as well as bringing us towards a *progressive personalization of consumption,* towards an aggregation of *transversal* expressive spaces (online communities, m-sites, reality shows on TV...) where we are able to satisfy our desires for a tale's appropriation and sharing. From this point, the experience can develop the vital energy of *transmedia* storytelling with the promotion of stories across multiple media that interact with

---

[1] Henry Jenkins, *Convergence Culture: Where Old and New Media Collide* (2006).

each other in a way that is even more evocative, integrated and participative to the audience. How?

- By creating publishing spaces that, being simultaneously distributed through multiple media, involve different and interactive methods of consumption for the different audiences of the project (even if educating them to its use).
- By making the consumer of each media asset autonomously develop the contents of the project, exposing himself and becoming *visibly present and identifiable* in the universe of the tale.

In fact, thinking *transmedia* doesn't mean just distributing parts of the story in different media, then strictly putting publishing restrictions and dealing with the shuffled parts on the table, as in a charming *solitaire* game. On the contrary. *Condicio sine qua non* for a transmedia tale is the continuous dialogue between the involved publishing platforms and the consideration of creative and consumer spaces that belong to each of them, necessarily *starting from the audiences*[2], at all times. In transmedia projects, the authorship is often more hidden than shown, and the responsibility for the tale is disguised in the story and its different uses, in order to consider – from the beginning – the WHAT and HOW of the tale as a function of the audience, more than the creator (storyteller, producer, promotions manager). An example?

One morning in June 2006 three hundred people all met together just outside the POW Entertainment studios in Santa Monica, all dressed-up as improbable superheroes, all armed to the teeth. They are there in the hopes of being selected for a

---

[2] It is a condition that partially modifies M. McLuhan's theory (*Understanding media*, 1964) that states "the content of any medium is always another medium" changing it into "a medium that is incorporated or represented within another medium", or even into multiple media positively combined in one single system.

new reality broadcast by SciFi Channel: *Who Wants to Be a Superhero,* created by Stan Lee, who is also the creator of *Spider-Man, The Fantastic Four, The Incredible Hulk, X-Men* and the whole pantheon of the "Marvel Universe".

The first ones to go are men and women who use their "closeted superheroes" on this occasion, because, following the rules of their favorite masked characters, the costumes should be original and *self-made*. Hence, the first ones to pass through the gate of the broadcasting station are: narrators (writers, communicators, scriptwriters) and creative people (sketch artists, storyboarders, comic-strip writers, actors) of fandoms and American communities.

> "Muscular teenagers and never-ending fanatics, art directors from Hollywood, pretty schoolgirls and refined intellectuals enter the structure where the selection is, while Stan Lee is announcing to the *Los Angeles Times*: 'we are not going to ask them to show us they are able to fly or climb skyscrapers. But each of these heroes has some powers, such as bravery, fortitude, honesty, integrity, self-sacrifice, altruism and the ability to adapt. These are the values we are going to consider'".[3]

How? By creating stories for the candidates to directly experience, individually or in groups. After all, the prize was very tempting – for these kind of fans, you know – and it directly linked the reality play with the transmedia: a comic book would be created on the basis of the winner's achievements and signed by Stan Lee himself, and a TV-movie would be produced and broadcast by the SciFi Channel. Previously, candidates took part in dozens of challenge matches and for 6 weeks they spent 24 hours a day in a mystery den, under the watchful eye of the authors and the audience.

---

[3] M. Giovagnoli, *Cross-media. Le nuove narrazioni* (2009).

From a commercial point of view, *Who Wants to Be a Superhero* didn't stake everything on the television program's success, but, in particular, on the feedback of the deep-rooted and *media-active* fans of comics, cartoons and movie heroes[4]. Narrators and creators who had always wished in life to not only embody their favorite superhero, but "Themselves as Superhero".

Following the narrative structures and stories that were useful for the show, the program was the paradigmatic example of one of the most innovative forms of the contemporary story: the *stunt-show narratives*, stories that make the specific audience of a media arena able to have direct experiences with spectacularly high potential. This happens because they are simultaneously distributed on multiple media as an anarchical and unconditional choice to experience them. Consequently, they are more touching and "truer than reality", and open up several possible *stories* in the articulated plot.

Thus, *Who Wants to Be a Superhero* is much more than the umpteenth reality show or a "*Big Brother* for the superheroes' maniacs". *Stunt-show narratives* today are also part of the most specialized forms for audience *entertainment*, because through them the physical distance between the narrative (stories, heroes) and the technological platforms (TV, web, comics) is transcended.

Yet, what are the most efficient strategies and operations to create this kind of narrative?

To enable the participation of the audience and the sharing of a tale's imagery distributed on multiple media, it is necessary to guide the different audiences of each medium involved in the project towards an independent use of the story, expressing clearly:

---

4 A. Haas Dyson, *Writing Superheroes: Contemporary Childhood, Popular Culture, and Classroom Literacy* (1997).

- short parts of the plot and the rules of the "game" you are going to play, clarifying the roles and contents you need to create in the multiple media involved;
- associations that link the multiple media in those areas of the tale that could work as easily shared *points of entry* for the audience;
- the basic features of the *narrative contract* that links the authors to the users, that is: the action space of audiences, both for the character's development in the story and for the solution of a problem, the reversal or confirmation of a point of view, etc.

An example for this case? Picking up in the "prehistory" of transmedia, the mixing of stories and tales of the first Disneyland, created in Anaheim, California in 1955, led to the theme park: the first huge world location that would host a promotional system, movies and cartoon launches through multiple media. At the same time, Disneyland in Anaheim was the prototype for the amusement park and a transmedia framework, the fruits of a Disney and ABC TV broadcast partnership aimed at the shows and events planned for the occasions of new movie releases (yearly) or the broadcast of old successful movies (every seven years)[5].

An efficient *fil rouge* made of gadgets, real scale masks and different attractions which let millions of spectators and thousands of young visitors to Anaheim feel as if they were sharing the same imagery or, as Jay Bolter and Richard Grusin write, they were physically and constantly *"surrounded by media"*.[6]

And now, here we are. In the space of a few generations we have technologized our bards and disguised our shamans that were created in five millennia of History. In order to *imagine differently* we have created and then made the media compete

---

[5] C. Anderson, '*Disneyland*', in: H. Newcomb (edited by), *Television. The Critical View* (1994).
[6] J. D. Bolter, R. Grusin, *Remediation. Understanding New Media* (2000).

with each other, and then with our imagination. We have searched for new, free territories where we could learn from storytelling and now we are exactly there. We are continuously spurred into action by new technological goals, in a non-place, following Pierre Levy's theory, at the edge between the commodity space and the knowledge one (*cosmopedia*)[7]. For this reason, "thinking transmedia" means: to face the remediation of our contemporary industry of information, entertainment and communications, getting ready for a "new creation each time"; for a *redistribution of the imagination*; and for a new artistic and scientific opportunity to communicate information and feelings that help the audience to continue developing.

Short Introduction to Transmedia Definition

A history about the definition of *transmedia* has not been written yet and scientific sources and academic research would be necessary to do it, as well as documentation, marketing plans, networks, broadcasters, and major media communications companies' promotions, which are all spread around the world. The following summary is not a scientific reconstruction, but rather an outline of the principal points that helped clarify the *use of this term* in the everyday life of (corporate and amateur) narrative, and in multiple media all over the world, both incidentally and intentionally, during the last fifty years.

In the West, the term *transmedia* was first coined by the American researcher Marsha Kinder, who wrote in her 1991 book *Playing with Power in Movies, Television, and Video Games: From Muppet Babies to Teenage Mutant Ninja Turtles* about

---

[7] P. Lévy, *Collective Intelligence* (1988).

23

"commercial transmedia supersystems." She was referring to the publishing projects of some globally important franchises distributed on multiple media.

Five years later, Paul Zazzera, CEO at Time Inc., was the first to use the similar term *cross-media* that was soon seen all over the world through the start of *Big Brother* (a reality show presented as a cross-media format by its creator John De Mol in 1997) and the unexpected global success of *The Blair Witch Project* (1999), as well as the creation of *Second Life,* which according to statements by Linden Lab (2003) included and "crossed" all the media within its virtual world.

The *transmedia* definition was drawn on during the same year (2003) by Henry Jenkins in an article in *MIT Technology Review* that was entitled "Transmedia Storytelling" and highlighted the basic differences between the experiences that were unexpectedly and randomly being diffused across the world. Meanwhile, thanks to the 2003 study by the researchers Christy Dena and Jak Bouman in the Dutch *Acten Report,* the definition of cross-media was being refined, while in the professional world, both expressions began to crossbreed, becoming even more difficult to distinguish. At the same time, quite a number of essays on the topic were being written all over the world and in 2005 I also wrote a book, the first one published in Europe, which was entitled *Fare cross-media.* I then held the first Italian *Cross-media # 1 Day* event, which to this day is still organized once a year in Rome with a focus on new trends and experimental projects in the transmedia industry. But the most official page in the history of the *transmedia* definition was written in 2010, after the industry adoption of the term by American cinema, thanks to Jeff Gomez and the Producers Guild of America, who finally inserted the title, "transmedia producer," in the list of credits for Hollywood movies.

If we move from the definition's history to the practice of transmedia in the world after its baptism in the Disneyland resort in Anaheim, we should go back to its genesis in 1976.

This was the year of the creation of the *Star Wars* saga by George Lucas, which started the transmedia model on a corporate level and soon transformed into a publishing group in order to produce and promote all the multimedia materials that were linked to the project. At the same time, this year was the origin of *text-adventures* – which are played by connected multiple users – with the release of *Colossal Cave* by William Crowther, linking it with the global growth of gamebooks[8], thanks in particular to *The Cave of Time* written by Edward Packard in 1979. All of these are examples of interactive tales through which new forms of *dramatic cooperation* were quickly being established between authors and audiences for the creation of plot and characters of the story.

There is another prior term, which is becoming more popular in the conferences and international meetings about transmedia: a term coined by the German composer Richard Wagner, who in 1846 was already talking about the *Gesamtkunstwerk*, that is to say a sort of total, comprehensive, universal work. His essay was the "setting" of a synthesis of the subjects involved in the future work of art, within the physical framework and the imaginative universe of the theater. This synthesis was not so far from reality, considering that the theatre spaces of a contemporary metropolis are even more part of the fabric of a city, through works and performances on interactive floors or by videomapping, augmented reality or soundscapes, walk shows and further forms of interactive storytelling. On the contrary, a fine

---

[8] The first work that was considered similar to the gamebook was the *Examen de la obra de Herbert Quain* written by Jorge Luis Borges in 1941 and dedicated to the tale of a novel divided into 3 parts that are linked through 2 "narrative bridges", each with nine different endings. The gamebook is a second-person narrative, with chapters that develop through different narrative options, depending on the reader's decisions. Its global distribution was marked by the creation of novels' series for young people 'Choose Your Own Adventure" published by the English Bantam Books between 1979 and 1998, in which the novel by Edward Packard, *The Cave of Time*, was the first work in the backlist, with 40 alternate endings.

distinction that is important and often undervalued when talking about Wagner and *his* "Artwork of the future", is related to his idea of authorship, which focused on how the artist had an "absolute responsibility for the planning and its realization" of the work, without devolving any creative space to the audience's contribution.

Transmedia Culture

Maybe it's because of a need for higher autonomy with the stories and characters they create, but today directors and authors who have contributed to the creation of the collective imagination are now choosing to create their own transmedia transpositions of their work. Products and content that are created for movies or TV are adapted and then distributed via cell phones, comics or books, on the web or as videogames, leading to a "freshness" and a generally positive brand image. Steven Spielberg cooperated for the creation of the videogame of *Jaws*. George Lucas cooperated for the TV series made out of *Star Wars*. Peter Jackson for the movie that drew inspiration from the *Halo* videogame series and, at the same time, for the realization of the game made from his *King Kong*[9]. Not to mention the Wachowski brothers, who even cooperated with their audience to create the script and direction of short animations, and the storyboard of comics that drew inspiration from the movie and the *Matrix* videogame.

If the creators of large global franchises are even more engaged in the development of a transmedia universe of their projects, then there is also an increase of spaces in which the audiences can reinterpret the imagery of the story. Above all, these "new narratives" are interpreted by the audiences as a

---

[9] http://www.cross-media.it

semantic basin[10], which is open to continuous crossbreeding, and as a *cultural activator*[11] that is able to incorporate different narratives and other kinds of constructions, even if things don't always go in the same way. An example?

This production model of Renaissance workshops can be corrupted by advertising factories, as highlighted by Lucas, as well as by the LOST creators, Damon Lindelof and Carlton Cuse, who worked to make the writing process of the TV series simultaneously useful to the creation of all the other official brand products as well, enabling *permanently changeable imagery* for the series. In this way, *LOST* gradually became a mobisode (the story is about a manuscript found on the island) and at the same time a series of console and PC videogames, a comic series, a book and a series of *alternate reality games* (*The Lost Experience, Find 815, Lost University* and more). It is the first large "transmedia bouquet" around a TV series, with numerous usable and playable, editable spaces for the audience, all of them characterized by a strong osmosis between *immediacy* and *hypermediacy*[12], with an endless exchange between the immediacy of the tale and its permutations and the obscurity and presence of alternate and hyperstructured additions, which are not always found in the audiovisual series, but exist in other kinds of media spaces (*hypermediacy*).

Similarly, a *two-goal structure*[13], which highlights the co-presence of two main aims in the narrative line of each character is used in all aspects of the series. In each episode,

---

[10] Gilbert Durand defines the *semantic basin* of a story as the relation between the life and the length of one's imaginary productivity, in: G. Durand, *Les structures anthropologiques de l'imaginaire* (1960).

[11] Analyzing *Star Wars* as a case of a cultural activator, Joseph Campbell defined this saga as a "monomyth, that is a conceptual structure that comes from an intercultural contagion of images and icons of the largest religions in the world" which is based on the narrative myth of the *travel of a Hero,* as you can read in: B. S. Flowers, *Joseph Campbell's The Power of Myth with Bill Moyers* (1988).

[12] For the definitions of *immediacy* and *hypermediacy*, ref. to J. D.. Bolter R. Grusin, cit.

[13] To see the definition of "two goal structure", ref. to. D. Siegel, *The Nine Act Story Structure,* "Proceedings of the Computer Game Developers Conference" (1996).

this is always linked to a sub-plot, which involves all the collectively experienced adventures of the castaways.

It's a TV model that seems to be even better articulated in the videogames related to the series, which go from graphic adventures to first-person *quests* or multiplayer ones with *plot-driven* or *character-driven* stories. All the games are related to the background of the characters, moving through the various media, through the present time of the plane crash and the flashback of the characters lives *before* the airplane crash. All of these are strengths of *LOST,* but what is the worst part of this transmedia experience? The *interoperability.* In other words, you can watch *LOST* on TV, you can play it, relive or collect it, but it is impossible for anyone to influence the story. The brand, in fact, does not include any room for audience agency that comes from the "low level", and its dimension, which is exclusively *corporate,* does not leave any room for the revision or modification of the tale. This is an aspect that is very important to the grassroots narratives of new consumers of Entertainment 3.0.[14]

It's a choice oriented towards editorial caution, necessary because of the great amount of "unmentionable secrets" in the plots throughout the series. From the authors' point of view, in new *transmedia culture* narratives, the social development and emancipation of the audience's role is strongly oriented towards the opportunity to use different forms of a tale by highlighting:

- your own emotional experience in spaces that are gratifying and can be directly and explicitly emphasized through the audience's involvement in multiple media;

---

[14] Here it refers to the distinction between a corporate dimension (whose leaders are the major copyrights' possessors of the tale) and the grassroots ones (which come from the "low level", undirectly and unprogrammed, by the users); this is the theory of Henry Jenkins in: H. Jenkins, *Convergence Culture* (2006).

- a deeper sense of personification in the tale, also through the tale's transposition on a performative level (for example, through "urban" actions or experiential marketing);
- a greater tendency to an emotional economy in opposition to the audience of traditional broadcasters. More active, attached and socially connected to the "heart" of the brand.

Following this way of understanding, in the book *E-Tribalized Marketing* by Robert V. Kozinetz, the author divides the participants of today's transmedia communities into the following categories by their *active involvement* and their *proactiveness: tourists, minglers, insiders* and *devotees* (from the least involved users to the ones that are most involved in the communication and in the brand content)[15]. Some examples?

In 2008, Coca Cola created the *Happiness Factory* campaign, a contest that aimed to create an animated movie with the active contribution of the users on an interactive site. You had to choose a character from the ones presented in an introductory trailer, then register in a virtual job center and you soon started to work in the "Coca Cola factory". At the end of the competition, through the contribution of all the participants, an ad of the initiative was realized. The appropriation of the narrative and the participation in the creation of the story were the users' task, but, at the same time, they were guided and helped to set the tale by the authors of the campaign who created an innovative narrative process that was protected by the brand. It was very successful on a media level, but not so appealing for the most active communities more interested in the *personification* of brands in the whole "transmedia culture", the Kozinets' insiders and devotees, that

[15] R.V. Kosinetz, *E-Tribalized Marketing? The Strategic Implications of Virtual Communities of Consumption*, in: "European Managment Journal", 17/3/1999.

are *cosplayers* and *fandoms* (though they were not the main audience of the campaign). Cosplayers and fandoms are examples of a *post-literate*[16] culture, which prefers active intervention in managing information and exposure to the horizontal communication of major companies and mass media. They are annoyed by editorial "leveling out" and, consequently, they tend to show their personal *èthos* through the tale. They enjoy creating their own stories, unifying fragments of information that will be shared among the few experts, chosen people, and fans that they are. The aim of their actions is to create a new and more personally imaginative mythology. But, considering the *traits d'union* between these two different groups, it is also necessary to briefly illustrate the great differences between them.

Cosplayers are "the saga of game-lovers, who transform themselves from passive users to protagonists through the person of the tale, changing their appearance through the use of clothing and behavior of original characters in the story"[17]. A narcissistic aspect along with a great competitiveness make cosplayers more sensitive to performances and shows than the actual tale. Generally, their narratives consist of photo books and reportages, photo-stories, videos and animated choreographies. Bright and sculpted hair, thin and plucked eyebrows as in Japanese anime, modeled clothing and extreme paleness of the skin, or even the extreme use of cosmetics to look very pale are all the signs of the desire to embody a brand and a *cartoonization* of a look; they strive for new self-

---

[16] U. Eco, *Apocalyptic and Integrated Intellectuals* (1978). As regarding as comics analysis, new media narratives and "post-literacy", also refer to L. Fiedler, *The Middle against Both Ends*, in: *The Collected Essays*, Vol. II (1971).

[17] Cosplay tendency was historically created on 1981, during the 20th edition of Comic Market in Tokyo, the most important international event for Manga and Anime, where some girls began to be dressed *Lamù*, the greatly renowned heroine and protagonist of *Lum Uruseiyastura*. After this specific context, cosplayers spontaneously developed on Web, through thousands of websites all over the world.

representations, which is typical of their generation and culture.

In comparison, the fandom audience[18] is more inclined toward the creation of written and audiovisual tales (text only, short films, cartoons and graphics) and the creation of imageries, rather than their *representation*. On a global level, this is currently the largest area in the creation of new transmedia narratives. And thanks to the web, you can explore thousands of fandoms. Fandoms can be found all over the planet and are continuously bolstered by the perseverance and constructive aspect of every member. They use open source publishing platforms for their tales and social networks in order to best keep their relationships alive. It's a daily experience of the *foundational narrative*[19] as defined by Brenda Laurel, which is based on legends, narrative cycles and plots written in order to explain the roles and hierarchies of each group. Keeping this perspective in mind, the basic elements of fandoms are:

- narrative voluntarism;
- strict internal rules (narrative ones, but also referring to the imagery of the brand of the group);
- testing (in two ways: anonymously and explicitly);
- opposition to external aggregation (for example, the aggregation that exists among the different groups who favor the same brand).

Fandoms are most often textual *fanfictions* and audiovisual *fanmovies* related to internationally-known transmedia brands. Some examples?

Case 1. "The Daily Prophet" is the title of a project created in March 2008 by a young girl named Heather Lawyer, an

---

[18] Oxford English Dictionary traces the origins of fandoms to 1903, but it is through the fiction and fantasy series and movies that fandoms actually developed all over the world,since 50s of last century.

[19] B. Laurel, *Design Research: Methods and Perspectives*, Cambridge, MA (2004).

online magazine with a strong group of about 100 fanfiction writers from around the world who are working within the *Harry Potter* brand. In 2010 it even became a "movie" thanks to the contributions of the magazine's editors. Both "The Daily Prophet" and "Potter War" were selected by a major company to help create the *We are Wizards* documentary, a full-length movie that was screened at the Southwest Film Festival; and, as Henry Jenkins noted[20], it was a powerful example of digital transmedia storytelling, especially considering that in order to be part of the "Prophet" community, the authors had to assume the identity of a secondary character or invent a new one (an *original character*) in the saga.[21]

Case 2. The 501st Italica Garrison is the Italian garrison of the 501st Legion, the greatest club of Star Wars Imperial cosplayers in the world. It is active, with performances, events and parades all around the world, and it has also begun creating successful online short movies and fan videos for hundreds of thousands of users, which have even been broadcast on MTV. A fun example is the video "Never Call Me at Work", which narrates the story of an Imperial trooper being harassed by his hysterical wife on the phone while he is on guard duty on an imperial cruiser, until finally a threatening black figure appears behind him, freeing him from his problem… *forever!*

In both cases above, it is clear that the aspect that stirs the fan-authors' interest the most is the limitlessness of the stories and characters that can be created, killed, and invented anew without any problem, or any justifications of the audience's suspension of disbelief, or with regard to the prestige of the brand. They are used to being free from direct censorship and accustomed to acting without strict respect of copyright laws or corporate interests. Thus, these communities of writers,

---

[20] H. Jenkins, *Convergence…* cit.
[21] www.dprophet.com/

creators and communicators are occasionally able to create forms of transmedia communications that are extremely *complex and original*. They are able to easily cross national borders and, often, become privileged interlocutors with the creators of major companies of the cinema, videogames and cartoons of their favorite brands.

But, in order to describe and explain this level of complexity, it is necessary to begin talking about projects. And Planning...

CHAPTER TWO

Plan Transmedia

Each story is set in an imaginative universe and each universe is governed by laws. The use of transmedia multiplies the imagery of a story and divides it into many technological and narrative ecosystems where it is possible to relate and experience the storytelling. Hence, the tale needs to inspire a *great curiosity* (or better, an aptitude for knowledge) from its authors, producers and users, and a certain inclination for all involved to easily pass from one platform to another, and toward the combination of different *languages*. In fact, entering an integrated imaginative universe, which is also distributed across media, forces the public to behave in two different ways, studied by Howard Gardner in his research on 'multiple intelligences'. They consist of:

— a vertical process, aimed at the *assimilation* of content that a single user will benefit from, while using the media involved in the project;
— a horizontal process, or *adaption,* that a single user will promote in his relationship with the rest of the audience involved in the project.[22]

The creation of a transmedia work or project must always ease the audience's access to the multi-media content and rouse a willingness of participation and sharing from the

---

[22] G. Howard, *Frames of Mind: The theory of multiple intelligences* (1983).

audience. How? There are four essential guidelines used by all transmedia narrators and producers:

- frequent *clarification* of small parts of the plot in the different media involved;
- clear *explanation* of the relationships among the different media, suggesting descriptive areas and expressions that can be shared by the audience;
- *presence* of repeated *hooks*, *bridges* and *links* between the media involved in the project;
- *adoption* of editorial strategies suitable for the involvement of the audience in the formation of the story in every asset of the project. These are based on dramatic features such as: conflict resolution, pursuit of the goal, reversal or confirmation of a point of view, evocative interpretation of the theme involved across media, and comprehensive, effective, and emotional strengthening of the tale.

However, let's start with an example taken, this time, from the experience of an alternate reality game. It all begins on the morning of May 18, 2007, when the face of the actor Aaron Eckhart and the slogan *I Believe in Harvey Dent* suddenly appear on hundreds of election posters in ten big American cities. *But* it couldn't have been an actual election… In fact, after 48 hours, the posters and brochures are brutally vandalized. At this point, the audience's attention is captured. The mysterious candidate's face now has dark circles around his eyes, ugly bruises on the cheekbones and a diabolic sneer. During the night, the word *"Too"* has been added to the slogan. Batman and Marvel Universe lovers are the first to understand what is happening and start to spread the news online. For everyone else, a phantom election website is already online (ibelieveinharleydent.com) and the mystery is revealed: Dent has entered the list of candidates for the District Attorney's Office in Gotham City, and he needs our votes in order to fight organized crime. Before this faux election campaign, rumors of a *Batman Begins* sequel had already started to spread. It would be, however, more than a year after the viral marketing's initiation until the release of *The Dark Knight...*

Another two days pass and another website appears- that of the most formidable opponent of Dent and the election posters' vandal: the Joker (ibelieveinharveydenttoo.com).

At this point, the imaginative universe of the tale is totally set. The movie's marketing campaign has just started the longest and best-paid *alternate reality game* (*ARG*) in the history of film promotion, created by 42 Entertainment with Jordan Weisman. But what is an ARG in practical terms? Michele Giuliani writes the following about *The Dark Knight* project:

> This was just the beginning, if using a specific jargon it is the "Rabbit hole" or "Trailhead" of a long viral campaign, of the innovative variation of the Alternate Reality Game (ARG). [...] A sort of role playing game in an environment that is consistent with the merchandized product; an interactive narrative that uses the actual world as a platform, simultaneously involving multiple media in order to develop the plot created by directors, or master-puppets. Thus, gradually, players will deal with a multitude of ad-hoc websites; in parallel with this, they will be involved in some live "treasure hunts" or they will create different events, physically speaking, in the actual world [...]. However, unlike a regular role playing game, when playing the ARG you don't have another identity and time expands through silences and unexpected new clues. Also the rules are not illustrated but they develop by practicing the game. [...] Everybody is aware of the fact that it is a game, but you interact with events and characters, considering them as an integral part of reality.[23]

---

[23] M. Giuliani, in: "Subvertising" (July, 2008).

A week later, the Joker's new website (whysoserious.com) urges users to download photos which show how they have vandalized the city or tormented their friends; above all, it urges them to take part in a new crime *game* "launched" strategically on Halloween night. In November, an online daily newspaper (TheGothamTimes.com) is 'published', followed by the TheHa-HaHaTimes.com by the Joker. The newspaper includes links to the Portal of the Gotham Police Department (WeAreTheAnswer.org), the bank that will be held up by the Joker in the trailer (GothamNationalBank.com) and photos of damage to the city incurred during the final pursuit in *Batman Begins* (GothamCityRail.com).

During the following months, the events lead up to a totally unexpected turning point. The death of the actor who plays the Joker (Heath Ledger) forces the creators to shift the ARG's narrative focus to Harvey Dent's character, who will, in fact, play Two-Face in the movie, another one of Batman's arch-enemies. Several weeks are devoted to the diffusion of *fake* messages sent by Dent via mobile, requests for online submissions to his electoral campaign and distribution of gadgets all over the city... and everything happens without involving the protagonist of the movie (this time his name doesn't even appear in the title). Meanwhile, the launch of the movie is impending, but there is still time to play one more game. One night in Chicago, the police (the actual ones) stop a public "Dentmobile" full of the attorney's noisy fans, while a group called "Clowns against Dent" posts some threatening videos on YouTube. Soon after, Dent announces a live web-stream press-conference, which was canceled at the last minute because the candidate was somewhere else. An mp3 file later discloses how in a restaurant (Rossi'sDeli.com), a policeman (FrankNotaro.com) took a woman hostage, asking for the protection of his family and his own life. It was Dent himself who negotiated with the man, first saving the woman, and then assisting in the man's arrest.

At this point, the marketing of experience gives way to the marketing of the story. The alternate world of Dent is the actual one of Batman. The evil face of the Joker on the Web is the tragic one of the dead actor. Grassroots video of amateur 'joker' vandals as well as more collective efforts, like one of a surreal duel on a racetrack between a Toyota F1 and Batmobile. The quests and trials promoted by the viral campaign are now replaced by *ambient marketing* sets, which reshape the urban landscape and bring to mind buildings and skyscrapers of the mythical Gotham; they are also replaced by *beamvertising,* which promotes the movie thanks to brilliant projections on building and monument facades all around the world. And now the time has come to tell the film's story. Time to let the characters talk, and no longer autonomously. Time to spotlight the "new" Batman, reaffirming the *anagnorisis* (or tragic recognition) and the historical message of this superhero created by Kane and Finger: the *homousia* between Good and Evil, understood as the two inseparable sides of a single matter (which is "doubled" through the comparison Batman/Joker and Batman/Two Face), life and death with only a thin line in between (as also in the narrative).[24]

Thus, something more than a simple "launch" of a movie or a basic advergame is created. The creation of a new imaginary universe – ARG and viral campaign before, transmedia launch after – is based on some of the fundamental narrative elements of the *semiosphere*[25] by Lotman (from the characters' point of view to the audience's anthropological journey throughout the project), but is always very attentive to the active role of the transmedial audience of the project.

---

[24] M. Giovagnoli, *Cross-media. Le nuove narrazioni,* cit. (2009).
[25] For a definition of *semiosphere* related to a text or a story, ref. to: J. M. Lotman, *On the Semiosphere* (2005).

Modeling Transmedia Projects

Presetting the "shape" of a communicative system is a fundamental operation in the creative and editorial process of distributing a story in new media. In order to reach this goal, the entertainment industry works with narrative bibles, interactive maps, flow charts, networked systems... These models of "knowledge representation" are adaptable to a movie launch or election campaign planning, to a *reality show* or a *mobile games* platform, an urban setting or a transmedia journalistic report, or perhaps to an integrated advertising campaign, etc... Moreover, considering the complexity of the communicative processes – both *simultaneous* and *asynchronous* – which are used today by transmedia producers, the most useful kinds of representation, in my opinion, stem from different theories concerning the "shape of the universe". These come from natural physics, quantum and astronomical theories, and in the case of a transmedia project they refer to two fundamental systems:

- one *flat* and *Euclidean*, where the forces (different media of a project) and the bodies that are subjected to them (contents of the project) move on a single infinite plane, depending on measurable and classifiable sprints (after the official closing of the project as well as during the "active" time of its spectacularization);
- one *curved*, where the forces (different media of a project) and the bodies that are subjected to them (contents of the project) move around and take on different forms, which are not always predictable, as in neural or particle tissues.

Considering the two communicative systems it is clear that, based on the definition, the *curved* ones are often more complex. The publishing contents and interactions between the different technological platforms depend on the shape of the curve shared among the authors and the audience of a project. The calculation of this curve comes in part from Albert Einstein's theory of general relativity where, in his opinion, the mass of bodies is directly proportional to the entity of *curvature* that is used.

In the case of transmedia, the *mass of bodies* depends on the richness of their contents and the media alterations of a project. The *motion* depends on the popularization process and the operational use (through the communicative system) made by each of the involved media. Finally, according to the ratio of the curvature, the use of time and length of the tale, a transmedia project can have two additional "shapes":

- a *sphere* (with a *positive curvature*), which is a system based on perfectly balanced communication between the various media, with content that is cyclically and repeatedly distributed, with frequent shuffling and interventions of products that live a "second life" in the multiple media involved in the project;
- a *saddle* (with a *negative curvature*), that is a multimedia system in which the mass of bodies (media contents) tends to spread out and enlarge, but at the same time, tends to disperse. As in the case of reports distributed on multiple media, they change and repeat until their tales become fragmented and poor.

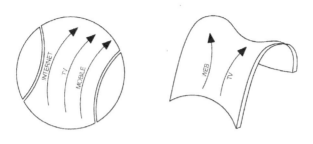

Img. 1 - Positive and negative curvature of a project

An example? After extraordinary success in the U.S. with its October 2007 publication, *The Secret* was on top of the best-seller lists in the U.S. and Europe within a few weeks, thanks to the use of a curved transmedia communicative system. The cover's *blurb* read: "Whoever you are and wherever you are, the secret can give you anything you want". Following the global success of *The Da Vinci Code*, *The Secret* was also launched as a low budget film, which used the narrative prototype of Dan Brown but focused on the emotional connection between the ordinary life of its audience and the dreams of its narration. The film, based off of the book, claims: "It has been handed down for centuries, fervently desired, hidden, stolen and bought, all thanks to a considerable amount of money. This very ancient "secret" was known to some of the greatest figures in history: Plato, Galileo, Beethoven, Edison, Carnegie, Einstein, and to some inventors, theologians, scientists and philosophers. Now the secret is going to be revealed to the world."

The online aspect of the project took these considerations into account. Over a few weeks, *The Secret*'s official website collected hundreds of stories recounting "my dream that has come true thanks to *The Secret*". At the same time, e-books, soundtracks and photos were given as presents to the online users. There were "dedicated" screenings of the film in movie theatres around the U.S. and it was sold online and abroad (thus, giving a negative curvature, or a saddle-shape to the system). Moreover, some of the stories sent by the readers were forwarded and then distributed, as well as published and spread online. This allowed *The Secret's* imaginative lore – although it was a low-budget project with no Hollywood stars – to quickly spread all over the world and accrue incalculable revenue. Hence, the case of *The Secret* is a paradigmatic example of transmedia narrative which used a curved narrative system with a sphere-shaped curvature for the book, and a negative curvature during the dissemination of its contents around the world. This particular case went from traditional media (book, cinema, home video) to digital (internet, mobile, social networks).

Point and Line to Plane

Christy Dena, the Australian pioneer of cross-media studies, was the first to notice that if a project integrates many different media platforms, it inevitably offers more points of entry for the audience. Having multiple points for an audience to get involved is a great opportunity, but at the same time, can prove to be very risky.

The *points of entry*, both primary and secondary, of a project have to be set and organized in the system with great attention, understanding their role and how they interact with the project's fundamental moments of navigation. The audience must not reach a project's primary point of entry in a traumatic or unsuspecting way, but rather by consciously moving towards it. Thus, it is necessary for each medium to identify itself and provide the pertinent information needed to explore the other platforms of the system. An example?

Since 2009, a mysterious killer has stalked the Italian Renaissance courts. His name is Ezio Auditore, and as in the usual case with avengers, he is very determined and very capable with both his time and his weapons. This allusive assassin is not on today's Most Wanted list, but is actually the protagonist in the *Assassin's Creed 2* videogame. For the publication of the second game in the *Assassin's Creed* saga, the publisher, Ubisoft, decided to improve and expand upon the transmedia variations that were created for the first installment of the game (with other games like *Assassin's Creed: Discovery* and *Assassin's Creed: Bloodlines* and with a series of three short movies dedicated to the backstories of the same imaginative universe, *Assassin's Creed: Lineage*. Soon a novel series dedicated to the various adventures of the protagonists, additional online videos, and a collection of action figures were released too. Each platform in a project, therefore, adds something to the game universe, and each publication provides a useful point of entry that allows further exploration of the story. All this is done with maximum autonomy, and above all keeping in mind the central focus of the project (the game) and its goal (recreation) in the eyes of the audience.

The most important narrative dimension of a transmedia project always consists of the way in which the audience interacts with it (*call-to-action*). Without a correct action process the whole system is bound to collapse. Therefore, the 'intervention principle' of a cross-media project's audience has three stages: motivation to act (*primer*), sense of the action (*referral*) and personal reward for the action done by the audience (*reward*).

A good example exists in an old TV ad that aired in 2004 by Mitsubishi titled *What Happens Next?* The commercial shows two sports cars trying to avoid objects that are mysteriously being thrown at them from the back of two trucks. The objects multiply and become bigger and bigger, until you see two cars sliding out of the trucks and falling on top of the two sports cars, causing them to swerve suddenly. At this point, the image disappears, leaving the audience in suspense (*primer*). A few seconds later, a website address is shown: seewhathappens.com. In the first six hours, eleven million viewers switched from TV to the web to visit the site in order to find out the ending (*reward*).[26]

The aim of the *primer* is to give to the audience a valid and specific reason to interact with the narrative. The Mitsubishi commercial did this by using a cliffhanger. On the other hand, the *referral* gives the audience useful information about how and when to come into the action. The information could be intradiegetic or extradiegetic, that is to say internal (like the commercial) or external to the development of the tale. Finally, the *reward* has two basic aims: give a direct response from the system (showing the audience that their actions have been noticed) and provide a material reward for their effort (consumption). "Planning a system of transmedia communication means creating stories that allow users to go from *the interactivity of consultation*, based on simple research of information, closer examination of media and the power of personal choice on the general completion of the project, to the *interactivity of conversation*, based on participation and the sharing of expressive forms and different technologies."[27]

Questions of Timing

In 1967, John Archibald Wheeler, an American physician, was the first to put a name to "black holes" even though he realized that they were neither totally "black" (because they emit particles whose weak evaporation can be recorded) nor were they "holes" (but dying celestial bodies, whose surface escape velocity is so high that it exceeds that of light, making them seemingly invisible)[28]. They are a type of cyclopean

---

[26] J. Jaffe, *Case study: "See What Happens"*, iMedia Connections (2004).

[27] M. Giovagnoli, *Cross-media..*cit.(2009).

[28] J. A. Wheeler, M. Rees, *Black Holes, Gravitational Waves, and Cosmology* (1974).

funnel with an intense and concentrated gravitational field that attracts everything during its rotation, even light[29]. Some of you may realize that this is the same Wheeler who, before becoming a pioneer in quantum gravity studies, had already taken part in the Manhattan Project in Los Alamos for the creation of the atomic bomb, and the Matterhorn B project for the hydrogen bomb. But... that is another story. Actually, Wheeler's theories about mass, charge, and angular momentum as well as those about the universe's wave function greatly contribute to today's transmedia studies. These theories are particularly influential in the creation of a hypothesis about the future of new narrative, as well as new technological methods of global storytelling.

One of Wheeler's most popular quotes is: "A black hole has no hair", referring to the fact that any object or signal, once consumed by a black hole, disappears without any chance of coming back. Even so, it leaves a trace because its mass and charge affects the gravitational attraction of the black hole[30]. How is this relevant? Well, what happens in a dark and atemporal black hole is comparable to the story of new transmedia: the collective imagination of oral, analogue and digital traditions that has been developed over millennia is now at death's door, but it continues to influence modern day storytelling. Black holes are ruled internally by "other" thermodynamics, which require adaptations and exceptions to universal laws. This also happens in the contemporary story: traditional paradigms and narratives are still used in the new transmedia interfaces, but they are subject to revolutions concerning how stories are perceived, imagined and created, not to mention the *horizon of events* or *laws of falling* bodies in the cone of a black hole... The similarities and possible implications are numerous. So, the following sections are

---

[29] P. Davies, *The Last Three Minutes* (1994).
[30] J. Bekenstein, *Black-hole thermodynamics*, "Physics Today" (Jan. 1980).

dedicated to different kinds of intervention – whether temporary or permanent – between one or more media platforms in a transmedia project.

THE STOP AND GO EFFECT

During the course of the story, one of the middle segments of a project is suspended, while other parts continue on, and then the stalled segment resumes its course as if nothing happened. For example, in a transmedia promotion of a movie, online trailers all around the world simultaneously disappear from the web as soon as TV and radio commercials are aired , and then return online a few days after the movie comes out.

THE DOMINO EFFECT

A particularly emotional narrative in one of the multiple media platforms or a particular asset of a transmedia project becomes temporarily more important than the others. This dominant asset changes the flow and direction of all other assets and acts as the dominant 'driver' until the conclusion of the project.

THE SPIN-OFF EFFECT

Like some satellites that take advantage of a planet's gravity to move somewhere else, one of the platforms in a transmedia project can temporarily attach itself to another medium in order to strengthen or revive its role or its content and continue towards a secondary goal in respect to the project as a whole. This is a strategy that forces the author and the transmedia producer to attentively and frequently supervise the comprehensive integrity of the system, in order to avoid collisions and imbalances in the distribution of a project's contents.

THE DOPPLER EFFECT

At a certain point during the development of a project, one of the media involved in a transmedia system changes its identity or language, altering its appearance as well as the comprehensive balance of the narrative. This works exactly as it does in nature with energy and sound: from an animal's cry as it comes towards you, to the different shades of a "color," or the temperature of the stars.

Another example? *Heroes* (2006), a TV-series created and written by Tim Kring, chronicles the lives of a group of people, initially unknown to each other, with supernatural powers. Since the beginning of the project, Kring planned for a progressive evolution of the story visible throughout all of the media involved. During the first season, for example, *Heroes 360 Experience* was launched on the NBC website. This online version was not very different from the series, and later changed its name to *Heroes Evolutions*, aiming to better explain the "universe" and "mythology" (the mysterious fantasy elements linked to the science-fiction and supernatural phenomena) on which the tale was based.

Heroes also used the "Doppler effect" from the beginning: different media simultaneously switched their roles (from primary to subordinate, or vice versa), and in doing so, they added to each other's narrative material, instead of competing with one another. In fact, the structure of the series, which was originally conceived as a series of *volumes* (the seasons) divided into *chapters* (the episodes), was very complex and needed a deeper analysis that would have never been possible in a shortened TV-series. Consequently (*the domino effect*), as the show progressed, five more web-series, a comic series (*9th Wonders*), a graphic novel (actually a long web comic in 160 episodes published by Aspen Comics after the broadcast of each episode), iStories and a serialized documentary (a *making of* for each season) called *Heroes Unmasked* were produced. Thus, it creates an imaginative universe appealing to any transmedia technogeek, while having a narrative paradigm, similar in some aspects to that of *LOST* (the survivors of an air disaster (artificial) and an island (natural) VS those endowed with superpowers of genetic or synthetic origins (artificial) and survivors of a (natural) eclipse.

This isn't surprising, considering that before writing *Heroes*, Tim Kring had worked for a while on *Crossing Jordan* together with LOST's creator, Damon Lindelof.

Transmedia Communications Systems

In order to define which relationships will exist between different media platforms, there are several models of representation that can be used. The designer or author must identify the most suitable model for the publication and technological aspects of the project. The most important difference between these models is the way in which the story is managed through multiple media within a project, a condition on which both the dramatic universe of the project and the variety of experiences presented to the audiences clearly depend. In this case, there are three different types of systems: *supportive*, *competitive*, and *omnivorous*.

THE SUPPORTIVE SYSTEM

In the United States in 1976, Ballantine Book published *Star Wars: From the Adventures of Luke Skywalker*. The book's genre, in some opinions, was too specific (both in science-fiction and in fantasy), and it wasn't able to attract the attention of a US best-seller audience. It was a proper publishing "flop". The novel was written by Alan Dean Foster and commissioned by George Lucas and was actually a novelized version of the screenplay, which was already in progress in Hollywood. Even the link between the two media (cinema and literature), shown on the cover with the quote, "Amazing movie by Twentieth Century Fox coming soon," was not able to save the book. This was partly due to the fact that the audience of the time was accustomed to the book being written before the movie but published after it. Since the beginning, Lucas had planned for *Star Wars* to be a transmedia project with a very large curvature (a rich nine-part story with many opportunities for audience involvement). Soon, this came to be true. In the wake of the movie's success, the book became a best-seller in America; it exceeded all expectations and contributed to the budget with which Lucasfilm would finance future episodes of the saga. Consequently, in the history of transmedia, *Star Wars* is the first case of a *supportive* publishing project (as *supportive media*), where the different media involved in a story are integrated, they share content and information and together invite the audience to participate in a series of experiences, quests and contests. They form links and bridges across platforms which allow for better communication and encourage fans to make *skill flows*[31] and to collaborate to create potential content for the project. The basic dynamics of the skill flow in a communicative supportive system are:

---

[31]According to Pierre Lévy (op.cit.), *skill flow* is the shifting and increasing of the sensory and emotional faculties of an audience, reached through the media function, incited particularly by the testing of new forms of interaction and execution, both personal and collective.

- switching from synchronous to asynchronous communication in the different media;
- using dramatic/theatrical teasers between one medium and another;
- using repeated content in the different media involved in the project.

THE COMPETITIVE SYSTEM

In the transmedia *competitive* system, different *ad hoc* versions are created for each of the media involved in the project on a technological, dramaturgic and consumptive level. Multiple media "split up their roles", and trigger antagonistic movement within the audiences. They rely on the autonomy of each individual medium in relation to the project, and aim at creating a more customized dialogue within each medium's own community. Since the creation of additional narrative versions requires further time and money and decreases the efficiency of the control exercised by the broadcaster, the use of a transmedia competitive system is often discouraged by the corporate management. Therefore it is more often used by independent productions. Some examples: A type of advertising available on the Internet is used as an alternative to a more traditional television-based one, for the launching of a new TV-format. Or the extra content of a movie preview is shown first to communities of cell phone users, or a level of a videogame that can be played online on the publisher's official website in preparation for the full launch.

Media components of a competitive system often *safeguard* short consumer and editorial segments that otherwise wouldn't have had space and would have escaped the control of their authors (with the consequent loss of their official format, *brand* visibility, profits for production staff and all the actors of the project). A good example from this point of view is the *in-game* narrative created for the DVD release of *The Ring*

2 (by Hideo Nakata, 2005). Using the same concept as the movie's plot (whoever watches a mysterious videotape is called and warned that they will be killed in a few days), a website was created (7daysleft.com) for each country where the movie was distributed. By submitting an email address and a mobile number, it was possible to terrify the phone's owner through anonymous messages, exactly like in the movie. Hence, a transmedia competitive system that used cinema, internet and phones ingenuously exploited the emotional repertoire of its different audiences by using the slogan: "Terrify your friends... it's easy and free!".

THE OMNIVOROUS SYSTEM

A proper *condicio sine qua non* of transmedia projects is the fact that a narrative should invite its receiver to cross the communicative system of one medium to another. From this point of view, the most effective communicative model is definitely the *omnivorous* one. In this model the different media are subjected to the presence of a central platform on which all the others depend (both the official ones and the ones autonomously created by the audience). An omnivorous communicative system is one that favors the creation of a common *agora* for all the authors of a project, and, above all, one that relies on what Umberto Eco defines as the "interpretive cooperation" of the audience. This is a condition that is part of the "text pragmatics" of all content of a project and is the real conversational *topic*.[32]

Moreso than with supportive and competitive systems, transmedia projects with an omnivorous communicative

---

[32] In this direction, it works the research of economic and planning models that, considering the marketing and communication experiences of the web, aim their interventions at the creation of vertical and horizontal communities able to build loyalty in transmedia projects.

system are based on a basic imaginative and publishing *pidgin*[33] which is shared between the sender and the receiver. For this reason, and because of its technological, economic and publishing aspects, the most effective medium in the omnivorous system is the web. In addition to being cheaper than other media, the web can foster communities loyal to a project because of the speed at which it can be updated, the high dose of creativity that can be expressed in its frames, and the opportunity to upload - thanks to a single publishing *tool* (panel) - the contents of all technological platforms of the project. That is to say that the Internet is like a tool for the delivery of content, and at the same time, it is a *retable,* one of the glasses in a cathedral, whose pieces magically dismantle and compose stories and tales under spectator's eyes. An example?

In June 2008, the novelist Paulo Coelho presented a great opportunity to his dearest readers: the web audience who for many years had been writing on his blog and following him on MySpace or Facebook. *The Experimental Witch* was a contest inviting filmmakers to create a new interpretation of his recent novel, *The Witch of Portobello* (2007), from the point of view of one of the story's 15 protagonists. The end goal was to create a *mash-up* movie, by combining the best fifteen short films. According to the project's rules, Coelho himself would be selecting the stories and original soundtracks through his MySpace mirror. The writer would also be engaged in presenting the movie in the most important international cinema festivals and world TV broadcasts. In addition to creative and promotional visibility, the project also included monetary awards for the selected short films and the best soundtracks. From a transmedia perspective, the project was

---

[33] *Pidgin* is an language that comes from the mixture of languages spoken by different people, who came into contact because of immigrations, colonizations, or trade relations. Considering the transmedia communication, it expresses a communicative code that is shared between the sender and receiver of all the messages and the contents within a publishing project.

soon spread among mobile and smartphone users, celebrating the imminent integration of the movable platform to the publishing proposals of social networks and Web 2.0.

Another example? In anticipation of the Italian release of *Bee Movie* (2007), an animated movie by DreamWorks, a different version of the plot (the adventures of a little bee that works as an attorney and takes legal actions against humans for honey theft at his species' expense) was used by the provider for the creation of an "educational" transmedia project that developed in two parts for *kids & family* targets. Two months before the release, in fact, there was a didactic contest for the students of primary schools, in collaboration with co-marketers and institutional licensors of the movie: McDonald's, Activision, San Carlo and the satellite TV broadcaster Coming Soon. In this transmedia model, " Il Giornalino", an Italian magazine, presented a special supplement, *Conoscere insieme* (Let's go to know One Another), that was totally dedicated to the bees' world. A special issue of the magazine, dedicated to the movie, was published soon after the *release date,* with an online contest, "Disegna e Vinci!" (Draw and Win!). There were subscriptions, didactic kits in 500 Italian cities and a "Monopoly-like" game as prizes. Up until this point it was a transmedia project based on a competitive system aimed at taking the audience into the movie universe, even before it was released. The day before the screening, at the Museum of Natural History in Milan, "A Honey Christmas Day" was organized. It was an *open-day* with a gigantic Barry Bee as the special guest. In order to allow the audience to return home after watching *Bee Movie* and keep on creating a "movie within the movie", *gadgets* and *giveaways* such as multimedia CDs, a leaflet promoting customized Happy Meals, TV advertising material and different *Bee Movie* gadgets were distributed. In this way, the system switched to omnivorous transmedia, based on a web platform and merchandise. But with this last example and its reference to the kids & family worlds, it is time to abandon the technological and publishing planning and go on to a new phase in the creative process: *HOW* to imagine stories that can have different versions on different media platforms.

CHAPTER THREE

Imagine Transmedia

You are in front of the black screen of your computer or comfortably sitting in a movie theater; or you're sitting in the bus, immersed in the crowd with your mobile phone in one hand; or in the kitchen, absent-mindedly walking back and forth, next to your TV there; or you're driving with your radio on; or you're in the bed with a novel on your chest. The entry medium to a transmedia system does not change very much, if we consider it as a door to enter the human imagination. When you are totally absorbed in the tale, at some point something simple and magical will be *triggered* and you will be *taken elsewhere*. The screen will light up. Letters on the page of your book will lose their ink and, as the Italian writer Italo Calvino defined it: our "mental cinema"[34] will begin and the words will mysteriously change into images. Radio sounds will transcend the sense that the verses give them and suddenly change into a tale. And this also happens to the endless 0-1 sequences of your computer…

---

[34] Italo Calvino, *American Lessons* (1985).

Simultaneously multiplying this process on multiple platforms, the complexity of management and the use of the story increases, and in order to "enchant" the audience, it is consequently necessary to properly follow the imaginative processes. Communication, in a transmedia project, uses two expressive elements at this point of the creative process: the *imaginative faculty* and the *cultural symbols heritage,* which are basic for the creation of the collective imagination of its audience. Hence, to do transmedia it is necessary to know the exact process of shaping the human imagination, in order to create, in the most effective way, myths, archetypes and symbols to distribute through the different *devices* available to the audience. On an imaginative level, Gilbert Durant defines the continuous exchange between the subjective dimension of the user and the more objective one of the surrounding environment as an *anthropological path*[35], comparing it to a sort of adventurous "path" walked by the user of a tale. In the case of the viewer, sitting alone in front of his computer or TV, for example, all the visual information he receives will be processed by his mind at high speed, as during a long run; the auditory information, instead, will be impressed in his short-term memory in a way that is three times more effective that, as in a brief trip, easing the passage from one image to another and working like the "water wheels of the mind". Adding to each other – the human imagination develops through the accumulation and specialization of the senses – visual and auditory stimuli will be ordered in logical patterns inside of us: they are called *scripts.* And imaginative scripts will be divided into neural *hubs.* This means that they will create a close net of deductive associations and predictions that will lead the spectator to the reconstruction and interpretation of the tale.

All these steps, which happen unconsciously in the audience of traditional media, use the associative property of

---

[35] G. Durand, *Les Structures anthropologiques de l'imaginaire* (1960).

the human mind as the privileged cognitive parameter and they "automatically" involve all three cognitive stages of our psyche (conscious, subconscious, unconscious). In the case of transmedia, however, the audience lacks a specific literary process and a high number of known scripts; this unawareness and disorientation necessitates a very direct point of entry into the system, not a highly complex narrative structure, and an easy scheme of interpretation, a sort of interface, in order to overcome this dystopia. The ability to reproduce an emotional experience is given, from our mind, firstly to our memory (conscious, subconscious, unconscious). Additionally, the emotional memory of a tale that is distributed on multiple media depends both on the individual culture (the ontological one) of the audience and the imaginative scripts that the author has been able to trigger in the users' minds during the tale. Managing a narrative on multiple media, simultaneously, always calls for a hard process of reconstructing the audience's mind, both on the emotional level and on the highly imaginative one.

Regardless of the use of its narrative system, a transmedia tale is like the sum of stories "split" into multiple media, but all developed according to the Aristotelian three-act structure:

PREFACE / First turning point > DEVELOPMENT / Second turning point > Story RESOLUTION.

Generally, the moments in which audience's imagination reaches its most productive points are the *incipit* and the first *turning point*, that is, the "Once upon a time" and the first plot twist that starts the tale. In those moments, anything is possible and the different media versions of the project are always "open" and always equally pointed toward an endless narrative. However, in correspondence with the *second turning point* (the transition between the second and third acts of the story), the *suspension of disbelief*[36] of the audience and its associative capability are even more passive, and the situation worsens going on to the final *climax* of the story. Undertaking this inverted process, from a personal experience toward the general one reproduced by media, the audience goes from the predicted-vision and imagination of the tale to active involvement and emotional participation. This is the moment in which the spectator actually becomes part of the story; when "something in him" decides if a tale is captivating or not, if it fascinates him or fills him with disgust, if it increases or reduces his desire to see it to its conclusion. And does it make him, if possible, feel like "surfing", together with the tale, from one medium to another. An example?

The Truth About Marika (Sanningen om Marika), an original and effective case of transmedia storytelling, is the title of a transmedia project created by The Company P. for the Swedish SVT TV broadcast and winner of an Interactive Emmy Award for the best Interactive TV Service Category in 2008. Presented as a "participation drama", it was a TV series, which, during its broadcast, changed from a traditional fiction into an alternate reality game that became very popular in Sweden. To that end, *The Truth About Marika* involved the TV, radio, web, social networking, mobile phones and most importantly... the Swedish at all. During this tale's fiction, in fact, the point of entry of the system was a woman's appeal to the audience in order to find her friend, who had just gone missing. News spread on the web and the hunt soon began throughout the whole country. Is Marika one of the 20,000 people that are still missing in Sweden today? Each news broadcast, each report and each reconstruction had public space in a panel discussion, which was reconstructed through

---

[36] *Suspension of disbelief or suspension of doubt,* expression coined through the narrative technique by Samuel Taylor Coleridge: it is the will of the reader or the spectator to suspend their critical faculties in order to ignore the secondaries insubstantialities and enjoy at most one imaginary work.

some actors of the same broadcast, simulating an actual disappearance. Meanwhile, the hunt involved online associations, search engines, online games, GPS, chat rooms, conflict rooms, a QR code, an official website (*Conspirare*) and a secret society (*Ordo Serpentis*), mysteriously linked to the disappearance. Fear, anxiety, desire to act: considering the success of the project, the most important parameter, on which the emotional sharing was based, was the audience's unconscious and subconscious satisfaction. In this phase of the imaginative process, the most important aspect is that all information and implications of the tale pass invisibly through the cognition of the common *pidgin* speaker (the author, the medium, witnesses or the project itself), the story (in the *fabula*, plot or scenes) and its receiver (that is he himself) in all the settings (the media versions) of the story.

The Nuclear Power of the Story

The complexity of the pidgin shared in a tale derives from all those narrative elements and signals that act as *amplifiers of meaning* in the multiple media of the communicative system. It is like a sort of energy, distributed and mixed, depending on fine ingredients that are able to blow up in any moment. I call this *the Nuclear Power of the Story:* a strength able to contain the whole energy of matter in its core and release it, if not controlled, as emotions and the magic of the imagination in our lives.

But from where does the strength and intensity to tell a story to an audience, or better yet, to multiple audiences simultaneously, as in transmedia tales, come? From the presence and combination of some narrative and imaginative components that are crucial for any tale: *universal synthetic structures*, *semasiological isotopes* and the *archetypal features of the tale*.

UNIVERSAL SYNTHETIC STRUCTURES

Universal synthetic structures are the basic coordinates of the narrative universe on which a transmedia tale is based; they are the signs and dimensions able to catch and transmit to the audience the *reference situational context* of the project. For example, Aristotle's three unities (space, time and action) or the characters' ways of expressing themselves and all the other conditions that structure the ordinary and extraordinary worlds of the story (so, the "rules of a game")[37]. In the case of *Truth About Marika*, for example, the universal synthetic structures were, at the beginning, the processes of feedback and notifications (written, broadcast or televised) developed for the audience; and only after, there was the *urban quest* activated by the authors, who were involved in disseminating clues day and night (with QR codes that could be photographed by smartphones, for instance) all around the national urban fabric and the digital space on the web.

SEMASIOLOGICAL ISOTOPES

Semasiological isotopes are iconic elements directly addressed, in terms of points of view and interpretations, to the subconscious of the user. To explain them easily, they are like symptoms of other realities, different from the ones on the surface of the story, or which are hidden beneath. In this sense, semasiological isotopes of a tale don't enter the narrative on an upper level, but it is like they have always been there. The result is to give the audience the impression of the right track, to properly face the challenge of use and, thus, be part of the game[38]. The use of semasiological isotopes during transmedia projects is necessary to accelerate the entry of an

---

[37] To better analyse the imaginary as an instrument for knowledge, ref. to: Anderson, J. R., *Cognitive psychology and its implications* (1980).
[38] M. Giovagnoli, *Fare Cross-media...* cit. (2005).

audience into the story and help the passage from one medium to another within the communicative system. In fact, the *immediacy* created by the subconscious' intervention in the audience easily changes into a sense of presence, and it quickly involves the user of the project, directly and with great chance for success. In the case of *The Truth About Marika,* the semasiological isotopes used were all the key-words repeated on the TV show and in the online pass-the-word developed by the authors, particularly during the young lady's and her husband's appeal, due to their desperation to find their missing friend. They were short messages that indirectly talked to the audience about one of its worst fears: disappearing or not having one more day (as happened while you were reading the tale) with the person that was beside you on the couch, who was very important for you.

ARCHETYPAL FIGURES OF THE TALE

While universal synthetic structures are the first available "bridge" to start the conscious involvement of the audience, and isotopes have to get the users' subconscious involved, archetypal features provide the project with the main emotional connection in order to have the unconscious participation of the audience, both on the personal level and the collective imagination level. The existence and use of archetypal features, that is, the primordial symbols shared among several cultures on the imaginative level, correspond to a crucial area in the communicative systems and the *homination*[39] of their stories. In the case of *The Truth About Marika,* for example, the archetypal features of the tale were

---

[39] About relation among time, imaginary and omination, ref. to: P. Lévy, *L'Intelligence collective...* cit. (1994).

the shape-shifter archetype by Jung, the "double identity" theme and the biblical prototype of Original Sin (also represented by images through the emblem of *Ordo Serpentis* and the name of one of the official sites of the project: *Conspirare*).

The Importance of the Emotional Competence

These are known as *media sensing*, that is the study of sensorial perception that is linked to the use and consumption of media, and emotional *labeling*, the identification and explication of the emotions during a tale. These are necessary activities for both the author and the producer in order to determine empathy and inference, or likewise, the irritation and disregard of the audiences in a transmedia project. Subjects that still aren't well understood by transmedia experts, emotional competency, sensorial literacy and emotional intelligence are decisive factors in the success of a brand or franchise that simultaneously uses multiple media to create or promote their contents and tales. The human brain, in fact, contains two "mnemonic systems, one for the regular facts, and one for the facts that have an emotional worthiness"[40]. This means that, before rational intervention by the cerebral cortex, which interprets the signals coming from our sensory organs and prepares our body for a rational reaction, in our mind "something" has already happened, and that "something" caused an emotion. It is a signal that is part of our emotional mind, and, in particular, of the *limbic system,* an area of our brain that consists of three elements: thalamus, amygdala and hippocampus[41]. *Amygdala* (actually there are two of them, one for each part of our brain) is a gland which is able to react to sensory impulses, starting in our body and in a fraction of second, innate physiological responses, caused by

---

[40] D. Goleman, *Working with Emotional Intelligence* (1998).
[41] J. LeDoux, *Emotion and the Limbic System Concept,* "Concept in Neuroscience"(1992).

survival instinct (even though in front of the seemingly undefended screen of a computer!): a real trigger for the emotions, whose function, in transmedia, is to worry or reassure the user at the beginning of a content or in the moment of transition from one medium to another, or from one language to another. The human brain, in fact, is composed of a thalamus, before arriving at amygdala, to which the perceptions coming from the sense organs arrive. The thalamus is a sort of *modem* that has to transform the language of the five sense organs into synaptic cerebral language. During its translation of the signal to the cerebral neocortex (*rational mind*), it simultaneously sends the message also to amygdala (*emotional mind*). Considering the latter is more immediate than former, it happens naturally; the emotional responses always precede the rational ones in our mind. This can have different, more or less undesirable, effects during the use of a transmedia project. In the worst of cases, that signal must be corrected and this can lead the individual (also meant as collective entity, or audience) to disorientation or disappointment. In the first milliseconds of perception, we unconsciously understand what the perceived object is, but we also decide if we like it or not. This kind of *cognitive unconscious* analyzes the identity of what we see and formulates a proper judgment. A judgment that, well-considered, is not in the amygdala or in the thalamus, but, rather, in a third organ: the hippocampus, whose main function is to provide an emotional memory of an environmental context, like that of the story. An example: can mobile communications and the web save TV instead of being its killer? Not satisfied by the outcome of its main series on the female audience, both adults and teens, Showtime production decided, in 2009, to entrust its series *Dexter*, which in the second season started to be criticized as a "bloody horror series with an evil protagonist", to transmedia strategies. Its plot is dedicated to the adventures of the most popular serial-killer of all serial-killers, a hematologist in Miami's forensic department; in the emotional mind of a part of the audience, this caused a negative emotional repertoire that the Starlight Runner studio of New York was charged, in the brand transmedia campaign, to transform in an ad hoc competitive communicative system for female consumers, using as the main products an animated series titled *Early Cuts*, a gaming application for iPhone, a role-playing card game and a very teen-oriented portal, titled *Follow the Code*. The result? A considerable TV rating increase and the most successful season for *Dexter*. How did they succeed? First of all, they gave an ironic taste to the promotion of the most paradoxical side of the series, the bizarre ethical code by which the protagonist commits his tortures. Then, decreasing the horror side of the series by using it just for Dexter's work as a member of the forensic department, regularizing and bringing out his background relation to blood, as a regular aspect. This is to say: deceiving the hippocampus and the emotional memory of audience by going straight to the thalamus, rational memory and anthropological structures of the audience's imagination. That's it.

Transmedia producers have to know the emotional processes of the human mind very well in order to be able to foresee and imagine solutions that are effective, satisfying and shareable among all the media audiences involved in their projects. Transmedia audiences, in fact, do not simply search for the creation of reasonable and exciting universes and narratives, but evocative universes and narratives, through which they can be spurred to an active intervention in unusual and curious media and cultural and communicative environments. As I said at the beginning of this chapter, in this sense, there are two basic components of the emotional provocation that are particularly effective. The former is the use of an emotional repertoire shared by the members of the audience, and it is important, in particular, for:

- the initial presentation of the project to its multiple audiences;
- the moments of deepest emotion and pathos;
- the relation to the eight main emotions (the primary six of anger, fear, joy, surprise, sadness and disgust, and two more, love and shame) to be transmitted on multiple media simultaneously;
- the moment of the official envoy (climax) in the multiple media of the project.

The second one is the emotional *labeling*, that is the power to "tag" in order to recognize and reproduce the emotions of the protagonists of the tale with the multiple audiences. It is an ability that humankind achieves during the very first months of life and its development depends on *feedback* processes, based on the parallelism among the emotional states and the mimic expression of the human body. A key role in the transmission of emotions in the transmedia is the one of *emotional contagion*, the immediate and unaware transmission of emotions from a sender to a receiver, who is inclined to experiment with them, as if they were his own.

Among the scientific theories that are linked to the emotional contagion, the most suitable one to the planning of tales distributed on multiple media undoubtedly is the *Perception-Action Model (*PAM*)*; in accordance with it, the empathetic sharing of a story or content can be more easily obtained when the representation of the emotion's subject in the audience is activated by a perception already held by the object/man who observes it. Thus, the subject (audience) gives its emulators (tale's protagonists) the sensations it has already felt in similar situations. This ease drives them to live and share experiences and thinking patterns which are gratifying and memorable[42]. An example?

In 2009, on the occasion of the launch of the 22nd edition of "Shark Week" on the Discovery Channel, the Campfire Society managed by Mike Monello, one of the creators of *The Blair Witch Project* created the "Frenzied Waters" campaign, defining it as "a transmedia experience that used influencer outreach, Facebook Connect and a website to bring the visceral terror of a shark attack directly to its audience"[43]. The web, social networks, satellite TV and the actual world all shared one of the most atavistic fears of contemporary collective imagination in a project that planned different stages for the involvement of audience, namely:

- the creation of a certain number of stories about people that died because of shark attacks (from the Second World War until today), with which any single user could identify;
- the creation of glass containers of clothes remnants, written pages and other proofs of victims' lives, until the fatal attack;
- the viral dissemination of containers in eleven U.S. cities, sending them to influencers, entertainment press, moviebloggers and radio personalities in order to popularize the campaign;
- the victims' profiles activation on Facebook, that can be signaled and shared on the social network before the program's broadcast.

Thus, an advertising campaign that used all the essential aspects of emotional competency in the transmedia: the emotional labeling during the TV presentation of the campaign (with trailer, teaser, pay-off), the emotional intervention of the

---

[42] To have an analysis about the role of psycotechnologies in the behaviour of media consumption, ref. to: D. De Kerckhove , *Brainframes. Technology, Mind and Business* (1991).
[43] http://campfirenyc.com

amygdala (for the audience's identification with the poignant victims' points of view) and the use of the hippocampus for the enhancement of context shared by the audience (11 American cities, the ocean, containers with victims' reports and their diaries...) throughout the project narrative. Additionally, the emotional repertoire of a generalist audience achieved through the viral campaign on the territory and the emotional contagion of the audience in the social networks (Facebook), ordinary receivers of digital sharing and personalization of stories, combined into a campaign which really succeeded.

Creating complex imaginative universes

Creating transmedia products means, above all, dealing with the creation of imaginative universes. And creating new worlds – original or pre-existing ones – is always equivalent to creating "complex systems of reference" which are able to enrich the traditional narrative through *further semantic stratum*. These operations, which are respectively defined as *world making* and *milking*, are useful to enhance a tale's imagination, taking complete advantage of its rules, myths and creative *spin offs*. It is a dual process that all creative people use daily in their work on a single medium, but which has a more complex and systematic meaning developing tales distributed on multiple media simultaneously. First of all, in the narratives that are part of multiplatform publishing projects, locations and characters change from one medium to another and they often have to be fixed or created *ex novo*. To create them, there are often narrators that don't know each other, who work at a distance of a thousand kilometers and operate after receiving recorded publishing inputs, using libraries of objects, character models and formatting rules prescribed by corporations or brands. For this reason, the use of fixed dramaturgic rules and narrative paradigms are so important that they have to be enhanced by the use of identifiable cultural symbols and key-tools of the collective imagination[44]. An increasingly common case is the transposition of the traditional comic world into the comprehensive symbols and languages and in the affective-imaginative repertoire of new digital media. An even more frequent case is the transposition of the comics world into the whole digital media universe of symbols and languages, in particular joining them with video games and alternate reality games[45]. An example?

During the winter of 2007, the Italian software House Artematica created *Diabolik: The Original Sin*, a video-game based on a comic which, over the years, has been adapted into the movie and cartoon worlds. The video-game's narrative space started from a painting's theft on a train and concluded with the adventurous rescue of Diabolik's partner, Eva Kant, who was apparently abducted for no clear reason. The video-game's difference – a graphic adventure that could be played in real time and could be changed at any moment, depending on the choices of the narrator-player – compared with previous versions lied in the creation of the same dramaturgic imagery of the tale through a variety of plot twists. Moreover, in the video-game, both the world-making of the new adventure and milking of *Diabolik*'s traditional imagery integrated with and complementing each other. In fact, the game can be played in two different ways: the first based on image and direct experience; the second included many secondary games and trials that were based on perception and choices made by the player. In this second mode, the game continuously used a graphical mix between game animations

---

[44] An excellent example of this kind of process is represented by the so-called *god games*, videogames where communities or worlds are managed and the game to adapts itself to the identity of the one who rules, and the user does not have to follow determined narrative patterns in order to create the universe of tale again.

[45] McGonigal, J., *Making Alternate Reality the New Business Reality*, Op Ed. "Harvard Business Review" (2008).

and comic paintings, commented with captions, balloons, and interval filmed sequences, in order to comprehensively enhance the imaginative context of the story. Finally, in both narratives, the tale followed objective shots, and developed considering the player's choices (the *choice option process*) based on experiential scripts and cognitive frames that were easy to identify (for example, in the choice of paths to follow or the operations to start, in order to achieve the aims of game).

To Perceive, and to Imagine

In his essay *L'Imaginaire* written in 1940, Jean-Paul Sartre analyzed the forms of reality's interpretation and the human mind's fiction, distinguishing between *perception* and *image*. The use of these two "monads" of fantasy today is a basic reading key for the creation of actual and fictional worlds and the locations of a transmedia tale. According to Sartre, in fact, during perception the knowledge shapes slowly, while in the image it is immediate. Exactly as a user can pay attention to an image as much as he wants, he will only find the things he brings to it. Unlike perception, in the image there is a sort of essential poverty. And, the image as image is describable only by an act of the second degree in which attention is turned away from the object and directed to the manner in which the object is given[46].

This means that perception and image operate in a continuous dialogue between the rational mind and the emotional one, enhancing or stigmatizing the different components of the transmedia tale, in single or many assets of the narrative. Sometimes there are mysterious short circuits

---

[46] J-P. Sartre, *The imaginary: a phenomenological psychology of the imagination* (1940).

operating in the mediasphere, creating "cases" of stories and characters that, like meteors, become mysteriously popular all around the world through word-of-mouth on the web. Thus, word-of-mouth is also a way to think about the image and imagination, and it spurs thousands of authors and users to mingle their fantasy with some pre-existing ones, and not just for fun. An example?

It's the 4th of November 2002 when a chubby fourteen-year-old boy went into the labs of a Canadian school and started to film himself with a broom in his hand, trying to act as if he was in a *Star Wars* lightsaber fight. Some of his schoolmates downloaded this film video on Kazaa, and in a few days it started the most sensational case in the history of broadcasting via Internet in that year. In fact, the video went viral on all the most important global online players (YouTube, Google Video, Crackle…) and little by little it started to get crossbred by the audience.

The Star Wars Kid's image (the nickname/tag of the boy) was cut and imagined through an "act of the second degree" by professional and amateur authors who transformed and inserted it in comics, or quoted it in important video-games (*Tony Hawk*) or in some episodes of the planet's most popular cartoons (*Family Guy*). The duel in Darth Maul-style was edited into hundreds of different situations based on images taken from action movies (*The Matrix*) and live action serials (*Star Trek*) among the most important ones in world entertainment. After billions of page views (in 2007 alone), the amount of money generated by the "Star Wars Kid phenomenon" quickly became incalculable. The Star Wars Kid's imaginary re-creation, even if it is extremely simple and minimalist in the content, testifies, in this way, to the great dramaturgic and publishing power of another peculiar narrative technique of transmedia tale: the use of parallel narratives, able to quickly describe the story from completely different points of view, both in the actual and virtual universe. Another example?

Molotov Alva and His Research for the Creator was the first virtual documentary created in the Second Life metaverse in 2007. The project was launched online through a video that said: "In 2007, a man named Molotov Alva disappeared from his house in California. Recently, a series of videos distributed by a anonymous traveler started to appear in a popular online universe called Second Life. Douglas Gayeton, the director, studied those videos and gathered them in a single documentary composed of ten episodes".

In the fiction, the tale was a "video-diary" of the protagonist, composed of ten dispatches of 10 minutes each, framed as the last witnesses of his life/Odyssey in Second Life. Because the project staked everything on the distance between perception and image, and the modified presence of the hidden user "by-laws" in digital features, the web began talking about it, and a movie was made out of it with the protagonist as the first person narrator; it was distributed by Submarine Channel and bought in 2008 by HBO, and was even nominated for the Academy Awards of that year for its originality and innovation.

The "Affinity Spaces" of the Transmedia Universe

To create transmedia universes, marketing and advertising techniques converge in an even more emphatic way in the primacy of experience, taking advantage of the world-making techniques that I have analyzed, and enhancing, most of all, those that James Paul Gee calls "affinity spaces" that exist among the different ways of using a story. The aim, in fact, is to let multiple transmedia audiences communicate as much as possible, to provoke a more active and privileged contact with the brand. New narratives based on intermediate affinity spaces overcome the limits of traditional stories, transforming them into real multi-sensory experiences. They tend to constantly research avant-garde technological universes and narrative experimentation to create them, together with the audience. Considering the creation of imaginative universes, the most effective "affinity spaces" for transmedia tales are *moving experiences*, *choice excitement* and the use of *expanded environments*.

MOVING EXPERIENCES

One of the most decisive requirements of the transmedia universes is motion, meant both as the fluidity of digital spaces and the simultaneous presence of different wandering users (connected or isolated). Dramaturgies that are based on a "nomadic" and dynamic consumption, make the use of a project through multiple media an experience in movement, first for scheduling the learning of a system's rules, and then for timing related to the management of narrative (for example, through physical movement or that simulated via mobile, tablet, GPS, console, controller...). Considering the creation of a narrative scheme, particularly in transmedia universes, these are the most important:

- the comfortableness of the tale;
- the plot's simplification (that is the use of mainstream and traditional narratives of the tale);
- the presence of pressing rhythm in the dialogues and stories;
- the explicit visualization of main phases of the tale;
- an aesthetics with tone and visualization (textual and audiovisual) that are not too elaborate.

An example? In September 2011 an emotional walkshow has been organized in the city centre of Rome, in Italy, to allow its audience to live for two hours in the ancient heart of Urbe Aeterna. The most evocative and transmedial essences of the project were two: the sacred (imperial and then Christian) and the profane (baroque and linked to the cinema myth of "dolce vita, or sweet life") both using a geo-blogging platform which was linked to a site with videos, soundscapes, 3D reconstructions, whisper talks and mini-documentaries; these were also physically accessible through the territory of the walkshow, disseminated with QR codes on panels and postcards. The tale developed by stages and almost "Socratic, or Peripatetic" experiences users could follow and proceeded, through the experimental use of multiple media, with the experience in movement of the physical crossing of two and a half millennia of history.

CHOICE EXCITEMENT

Among the most crucial functions of an interactive tale, the increase of attention to and enhancement of the decisive power of the audience are the basic dimensions in transmedia narratives. In particular, in tales based on choice excitement, there is not only a different narrative choice corresponding to each of the user's choices (as for example, in the role playing games, gamebooks or videogames), but the results of those choices prove more or less significant, because they are more or less effective in having a direct influence on all the basic elements of the story. For this reason, choice excitement is a way to manage the tale that requires simplified and universal platforms, servers and high-quality graphic tools, able to ensure effective, gratifying and impressive experiences to authors, participants and the audience. Finally, considering the dramaturgic point of view, in stories that "stake everything" on the choice excitement of different audiences of media involved in a tale, the following are fundamental:

- effective choice-autonomy;
- a seemingly provisional aspect of the general pattern of the tale, which has to be linked to an actual flexibility of the main narrative sequence in the imaginative universe of the stories;

- the audiences' direct and unanimous experience of trials faced by characters, and basic stages of the story.

An example? *Life-Size Games* are games and experiences directly animated by the audience within interactive spaces, depending on gestural or sound choices, linked to action-narratives. These vary from roughly ten-meter floor-puzzles or 3D animations, to the transfer of video-games into urban spaces to holograms and movie theaters changed into locations for alternate realities, played personally or by teams of users. Even more often, however, the transmedia audiences, based on choice excitement, aspire not only to become users, but also creators of content, directly taking part in the mythopoeia promoted by the narrative. Another example for this case?

In *The Horrors* web reality shows, distributed by Stream.tv in 2008, video broadcast online live from a house that was thought to be infested by ghosts, were, together with a *chatroom*, open 24 hours a day and reserved for the spectator community, lovers of ghosts, ectoplasms and similar people[47]. In this way, the inexorable static aspect of images (because of the empty and mute environments, experienced in the continuous expectation of moving objects, suspicious sounds, etc.) was broken by the ability to simulate and pre-tell the tale through the real-time communication of its fans, who were involved in meeting each other, making minimal choices, taking part in extempore contests, and entertaining themselves by chatting, waiting for the final beat of the tale: the ghost's appearance. Thus, more talkers than passive spectators, the game players immediately moved their attention from

---

[47] To have an analysis of TV reality narratives used for a specific "genre" of tale: C. Freeland, C., *Ordinary Horror on Reality TV*, in: *Narrative across Media: The Languages of Storytelling*, 2004.

emulation to self-identification with protagonists of the tale, just as happened, a year later and also in the movie theater, with the worldwide success of low budget movie *Paranormal Activity*, by the Israeli director Oren Peli. In the meantime, it passed from *on demand* consumption of narrative to the *on my idea*'s one.

EXPANDED ENVIRONMENTS

Aristotle writes, in Chapter VI of *Poetics*, regarding the tragic tale's nature, that it is just the "imitation of an action". If applied to transmedia narratives, this axiom is most effective within universes of the tale based on so-called expanded environments, "augmented" real or digital places, where "to live" is the same as creating a tale by using dynamic technologies like walled gardens, augmented reality platforms and tools, devices and consoles provided with movement sensors able to react to vector forces and orientation in the space. On a dramaturgic level, expanded environments are characterized, above all, by:

- a space that is an active part of the narrative;
- plots or stories directly organized by the action/reaction of the audience with the environment;
- a tendency toward community and interpersonal communication, inside and outside the environment;
- the disruption or re-creation of dimensional couples typical of space interpretation: open/closed, actual/virtual, natural/fictional, and story settings.

An example? The Canadian Hololabs Studio launched, in 2011, one of the many iPhone applications dedicated to augmented reality. But this one, named *MixAR*, had something special. It was not an application aiming at re-considering the space in an exponential way or displaying invisible things in the surrounding space, but to create a new space "that will enable users to create 3D objects in an augmented reality without any coding knowledge". Not only that, but *MixAR* could add some pretty interesting special effects like the 3D title effect used in Fox's show *Fringe*. The object/marker can be attached to a person, for example, and move with the subject. Here the integration with other media, web and, in particular, social networks begins, because, above all, the system "brings users the ability to snap pictures of an object and watch it turn into a 3D model that can later be overlaid in AR and recorded as mini-movies". It means to proceed from actual frames to digital ones, going through the direct co-creation of the imaginative universe of an audience inside and outside the arena set for the tale.

CHAPTER FOUR

Narrate Transmedia

If all the *Iliad*'s Homers, all the Egyptian scribes, all the authors of *Panchatantra* and of the *Old Testament* had had the Internet, what would be the narrative canon to form contemporary narratives today? Or, if the European artists and humanists working during the 14th and 15th centuries could have used a laptop, smartphone or digital camera to share the results of their research with Church libraries or the courts of the European Renaissance, what narratives, what "anthropological basis of imagery" would we be discussing now?

These questions, however provocative or paradoxical they appear, call immediately forth an inescapable *condicio sine qua non* within transmedia storytelling; that it is always collaborative rather than exclusive, choral rather than individual, heterogeneous rather than orderly.

It is a "constellation of texts and works" continuously demanding synergistic actions from its authors in the creation of the myths and the universes of the stories, while it is also the territory of technologies that enable accessible editorial platforms and tools for the distribution and interactive fruition of these stories.

From a contemporary point of view, the most recurrent transmedia storytelling strategies and the dramaturgic elements that have proven to be the favorite of authors and audience are: the narrative theme, the author's narrative voice and the audience's perspective which work together to form *two goal structures* with the reconstruction of the *anthropological path* made by the audience during the narration. In the tradition of transmedia communications, there are six pillars:

- *theme* (i.e. the deepest meaning and the implicit message of the tale); the theme of a tale is not explicitly told during the narration itself, but is related through the universal synthetic structures of the imagery, hidden in the story's framework. An example? In 2009, for season two of *True Blood*, a TV series created by Alan Ball that follows the adventures of vampires who are well-integrated into American society thanks to the invention of a synthetic type of blood that makes them apparently innocuous, HBO worked to expand the show's audience by launching a transmedia marketing campaign. This started as an online alternate reality game which centred aroundBloodcopy.com, and spread out across social networks (Twitter, Facebook, YouTube and MySpace,) and through an online forum on the HBO website (with an exclusive interview with Samson the Vampire). Some people received plastic syringes with synthetic blood, and they even commercialized a True Blood Carbonated Drink. Moreover, an American Vampire League was created to support vampire rights, while debates about whether or not American people wanted vampires living in their neighborhood were held in fictional newspapers and on TV. All of this along with a generous display of sharp vampire canine teeth and blood and without ever mentioning the theme of the series: integration and fear of diversity and confronting the dark side inside of us;
- the author's point of view should be invisible, but often manifests itself outside the project framework. This is

why only the insiders know of the few professional figures working as authors, even in a large transmedia global franchise;

- the point of view of the *narrative voice* is of some relevance when it is projected on to the audience in order to get them involved to help represent it and form a loyalty to it. As John Steinbeck wrote, "We are lonesome animals. We spend our life trying to be less lonesome. And one of our ancient methods is to tell a story". An example? In the *Big Brother* reality show, the audience's interest materializes when the "favorite character" begins to undergo confrontations with the other housemates. Once the favorite character is out of the scene, the audience's need for sharing experiences will lead them to select a new housemate as its beloved, similar to the former albeit with a different point of view about the story;

- the audience's point of view should be entrusted to a fixed medium to best ensure the effectiveness of the project's main narrative. As formerly said about the building of the imaginative universe of the story, this is vital in order to consolidate the *pidgin* language between author, project and audience. In the same manner, the portraits of characters are not to be defined by the narrative at the beginning of its journey, but further on toward the end of the narrative, both for the sake of the character's own cultural and educational background and for the sake of their identity and archetypical role. In order to do this you need secondary stories, like was done with the character of Mary Jane Watson in *The Amazing Spiderman* by creating the comic romance *Mary Jane Loves Spiderman*;

- in the *two goal structure*, where the protagonist starts focused on something and then, in the course of the narration, discovers he has to reach for something else more valuable or simply more risky: different media

have to take care to hold this in trust, in order to enhance the value of each of the goals across the steps of the narrative, both from the point of view of the characters and from that of the multiple audiences of the story. An example? In James Cameron's *Avatar*, the protagonist, Jack Sully, is a paraplegic marine who fights for himself (he betrays the Pandorians in order to regain the use of his legs) and at the same time for a better world (he merges into being one of the Na'vi). In the movie's marketing campaign Cameron himself admitted that such an ambiguous protagonist might have been a little disorienting for the public. «It's a very difficult proposal in our modern marketing world», commented the director, who also admitted that the movie, «put pressure on us to create the equivalent value of an existing brand without being an existing brand.» This is also the reason why the first choice of the *Avatar* campaign was to launch a 15-minute free preview of the movie dedicated exclusively to the discovery of the hero of the story, a "journey" which was also already playable in the videogame inspired by the movie, and with the toys and the action figures of the characters which Mattel enriched with augmented reality features;

- the reconstruction of the "anthropological path" made by the protagonists of a transmedia narrative must mirror itself at different stages in the different media. This helps stimulate a stronger desire for participation and cooperation amongst the project's different medial audiences.

With these pillars constant and present in all transmedia narratives, the other techniques discussed in the following pages help serve as tools for the author and the transmedial producer and encompass the dramaturgical, the imaginative and the emotional components of a narrative that can be additive and complementary to the pillars above. Most of all, it is possible to apply them to the whole communicative system of a transmedia project, or to a single narrative unit within the project.

Moreover, considering that the basic interactivity and complexity of transmedia narratives always involve different authorial forms, acting simultaneously or at different times, in the transmedia storytelling, it is possible to subdivide these tools and techniques according to two basic narrative solutions shared with the public: one participative and one synergistic.

Participative Narratives

Participative transmedia narratives use stories created by single individuals who set their tales within larger narrative frames taken from literature, entertainment, cinema, videogames, television, advertising, comics and the web. Their aim is to involve the audience and enhance the value of their contributions after the release of a transmedial product or work. The most important narrative requirement of a story is *sharing*, as devised by both authors and corporations within "protected" environments and, usually, in a non-profit scheme. Narratives concentrate all their focus on the work and the author is often invisible, hidden behind a nickname.

From a historical-chronological point of view, massive and participative narratives represent one of the "oldest" forms of transmedial narratives and their history has close to half a century of tales. There are two fundamental limits to participative and massive narratives: not being able to effect the narrative, and the *élitis* nature of the construction of plots and characters. A participative narrative is untouchable once distributed (all you can do is carry it on or add to it with another narrative); this fundamental condition makes participative narratives an excellent instrument for those transmedial projects based on supportive narrative systems, while making it a weapon in competitive ones. Moreover we can identify some common features of all participative narratives:

- the use of simple editorial platforms (with access barriers to prevent the audience from influencing the authors' artistic expression);
- the presence, within author groups, of solid friendships, even for a short time;
- the presence of informal tutoring, constantly occurring between aficionados and newcomers in the narrative stream and experience;
- the presence, in the corpus of narratives, of authors strongly inclined to nomadism and migration.

The forms of participative narrative analysed in the following paragraphs, which are among the most effective and most used in transmedia narratives, are: fanfiction and fanmovies in entertainment, nanopublishing and blog-narratives in communication, and adbusting and subvertising campaigns in advertising.

FICTION, FAN & ENTERTAINMENT

Fanfiction is produced by independent users or narrators by re-creating or altering stories taken from television series, cartoon, comics, TV movies, videogames, etc. The imaginative area and the emotional repertoire exploited by fanfiction in its stories are therefore always ready-made, even though they can be renewed and modified by authors both in the textual (*fanfiction*) and in the audiovisual (*fanmovies*) form. There are three standard *tones* for narratives: realistic, verisimilar or absurd (which can in turn be divided into ironic and comic)[48]. The fanfiction tradition goes back to the popular rewriting, by passionate readers of both high and low cultural background, of romance and "genre" narratives emerging between the 19th and 20th centuries, with stories inspired mainly by noir and adventure novels. More recently, the Internet has made possible the proliferation of archives and authors' communities, erasing the costs of publication for the public, so that currently we can count several narrative sub-genres within fanfiction[49]. Narratives are classified according to how true they are towards the narrative's reference canon (the Middle-Earth in *The Lord of the Rings*, for instance; Springfield in *The Simpsons*; Gotham City in *Batman*, and so on…). In this case, as Henry Jenkins has written, the fan culture is dialogic rather than destructive and collaborative rather than contrastive[50], and:

"The encyclopedic ambitions of transmedia texts often results in what might be seen as gaps or excesses in the unfolding of the story: that is, they introduce potential plots which can not be fully told or extra details which hint at more than can be revealed. Readers, thus, have a strong incentive to continue to elaborate on these story elements, working them over through their speculations, until they take on a life of their own. Fanfiction can be seen as an unauthorized expansion of these media franchises into new directions which reflect the reader's desire to *fill in the gaps* they have discovered in the commercially produced material".[51]

---

[48] The erotic register is strongly present, particularly in Japanese fanfiction or in that inspired by oriental themes, in reference to, mainly, manga and anime, with heterosexual and homosexual variations.

[49] M. Hills, *Fan Cultures* (2002).

[50] H. Jenkins, *Fan, bloggers…* cit.

[51] http://www.henryjenkins.org/2007/03/transmedia_storytelling_101.html

The forms of fanfiction that do not involve alterations to the original structure of the subject are called *canon,* and are faithful to the situational universe of the story, the characters' outline and the tale's continuity. According to a fanfiction tale's length, we can find the *drabble* (text up to 110 words), the *flashfic* (between 111 and 500 words) and the *one piece,* or *one shot* (more than 500 words). A story can be continued by the same author or, as it is with Round Robin Stories (RSS), by different authors. Among massive participative narratives, the canon stories are those with the lower degree of authorial intervention; as a consequence their use in transmedia projects is limited to, at most, contests connected to brand or franchise promotion. There are other forms which involve alterations to the original canon: the *Alternate Universe,* "lived" by the characters themselves albeit set in alternative worlds to the original one, and, the contrary *Out of Character,* where the setting stays unchanged and the characters vary, either through the introduction of new protagonists and favorites (*original character*), or through the introduction of heroes and protagonists from other tales (*cross-over*) or of real-life stars (*real person*)[52]. If the narrative is set before or after the original, especially referring to sagas and serial stories, we then have *pre-series* and *after-series.* Finally, those narratives which exploit an alteration of the original events of the brand, in order to create an alternative plot to the standard, are called the *What if.* This would be the case of *alternate history*[53] or *one shots,* which only present "closed" variations of the tale.

An example? My first job in the world of transmedia was that of editor-in-chief for the web and mobile section of the Italian edition of *Big Brother* (*Grande Fratello*) in 2002. That was a peculiar season for the show, I remember: as the finale approached, the audience response started to die down, mostly

---

[52] http://it.wikipedia.org/wiki/Fanfiction

[53] The first definition of di *alternate history* (in English, differently form Spanish, Italian, German and French it is not used the Greek origin word chronos prefixed by the negative "u") dates back to the 1876 Charles Renouvier pamphlet *Uchronie (L'Utopie dans l'histoire).*

due to the presence of many other reality shows in the Italian broadcasters' schedules. Compared to other formats such as *Survivor* or *Operation Triumpho*, the *Big Brother* housemates were "performing" much less, and their weekly challenges were hardly comparable to the hard trials of would-be castaways or singers. How then to give the narrative a different angle, so it would better succeed? In those years, I was doing my PhD on the "contamination between narrative and iconography in medieval literature and theatre" and I suggested to the authors a possible solution to the problem: a remake of Giovanni Boccaccio's *Decameron*! The analogies with Boccaccio's collection of novellas seemed to me so clear that it should have been impossible that nobody had yet thought about it. In the *Decameron*, ten young people were locked up in a villa just outside Florence in 1348 to shelter from the plague, and to entertain themselves, they started to tell each other a tale around a common subject. So was *Big Brother* not the same narrative framework-- the "House", the isolation from media, 10 candidates, the daily subjects? The idea was accepted and in the following show the housemates showed up in front of the cameras dressed up as medieval ladies and pages and challenged each other to tell a story. The result did not go anywhere near Boccaccio in terms of quality, of course, but the audience appreciated the ironic note of the exhibition so much that it generated several fanfictions linked to the different characters, that were interpreted and mocked from then on in many different ways.

Moving on to *fanmovies*, the distinctions between possible narrative forms are less rigid and often imitate filmic narratives. According to the length of the work, we have *shortmovies*, *fanfilms*, and *fanmovies*; to those artistic forms, we must add simulations of commercially oriented *teasers* and *trailers*. Then there are secondary formats based on entertaining and contradictory purposes, like *trials* and *action figure fanmovies*, which are videos dedicated to trials or attempts to imitate the brand characters with toys or puppets. The strength of the narrative lies in its originality and interactivity, whether it is live action or a toy reconstruction, whether there is a complex 3D set or an improvised location in stop motion. These films are shared through the fandom and online communities, not through official websites or web archives, as in the case of the textual fanfiction, but in the broader arena of online broadcasters, and are then spread by social networks. An example is the irreverent videos made by Trekkers, fans of the *Star Trek* TV series, ranging from Captain Kirk's romantic honeymoons with Vulcan officer Spock[54], to performances of rap bands whose intent is that of transforming the *Enterprise* control station into a location for interstellar video and music contests. More and more original and participative stories are now leading corporations to avoid censoring those narratives, but rather to welcoming into their creative branches those professionals who were formerly part of the fandom: the technofreaks and fanfiction authors.

NANOPUBLISHING & BLOG-NARRATIVES

The revolution that happened in journalism and infotainment between 1998 and 2001 has changed the role and modalities of information within the culture of transmedia projects. Today, the emergence of nanopublishing, citizen-journalism and blog-narratives on textual (blogs), audiovisual (vlogs) and mobile (moblogs) platforms offer audiences more accessible and interactive spaces. *Posts* (short comment articles published on blogs and social networks) and *pods* (reports published on web TV, mobile TV and Ip TV platforms) are participative and massive narratives which are published, shared and commented upon on a daily basis, mainly online

---

[54] P. Frazer Lamb, D. Veith, *Romantic Myth, Trascendence, and Star Trek Zines*, in: D. Palumbo (ed.) *Erotic Universe: Sexuality and Fantastic Literature* (1986), cited in H. Jenkins, *Fan, bloggers...*cit.

and under a merely user generated perspective, involving a non-stop technological and linguistic renewal. These conditions make them extremely useful when concerned with transmedia projects, containing in their framework quick and engaging updates, discussion and in-depth areas, viral marketing or human relief actions based on the power of content and message, as well as on the active contribution of the *consensus culture*. An example?

On the occasion of the Haiti earthquake in January 2010, the American Red Cross managed to raise 22 million dollars by the Monday following the disaster, thanks to a huge transmedia campaign in which The White House and the Corporation for National and Community Services took part. The main asset of this omnivorous system was mobile, with a text-to-give campaign whose testimonials included, among others, Michelle Obama. The message was very simple: "Send A Message & Save A Life, Donate $10 To Red Cross Haiti Relief, Text Haiti To 90999", yet a rich network of broadcasters and media companies all over the world joined in in support. In Chicago alone, just to mention a case, eleven TV networks, nine radio stations and two newspapers got involved within a few days. In the first 24 hours from the event on the Red Cross official website and on its social network profiles, millions of users and companies set themselves into action in order to raise funds, giving their contribution in the form of messages, short articles and comments which gained the project further donations. On the American Red Cross YouTube channel the first video on the condition of the island – five hours after the earthquake – was published. In the following days more reports and in-depth analyses from all over the world were uploaded. On the social networks, meanwhile, as Gloria Huang, social media specialist for ARC, declared, «On Facebook we had tons of fans, and there were a lot of discussions and forums where volunteers from previous campaigns were offering tips and advice to and answering the questions of those interested in volunteering for the Haiti relief efforts; the Twitter account, instead, remained a source of news, links to donation pages, and updates from the ground. And on the Red Cross' main blog, firsthand accounts, photos, and videos have been posted with unerring regularity»[55]. A vast amount of agile content in a blessed network, sharing web, mobile and social network content as never seen before.

BRAND NARRATIVES

In marketing and advertising campaigns, today, the main features of a transmedia brand or franchise can be turned into narrative matter for participative authors who, on their own initiative, decide to manipulate those contents in order to make them personal, or create new narratives independent from the original. The most widespread examples under the participative perspective are *permission marketing*[56] and *viral marketing* which, more than other contemporary forms of promotion, allow corporations to overcome the *information overload* in contemporary advertising and to actively involve the public in simultaneously multi-articulated narratives. But, when new types of narrative get close to marketing, advertising and other narrative forms which serve the promotion of goods or services, the modalities of creation and intervention might connote in a positive (*brand stories*) or negative (*adbusting* and *subvertising*) way. Starting from the former, participative brand stories mainly enhance the value of:

- a product's name and brand image;
- a brand's overall image and knowledge, including ideas, attractiveness and its consumers' "historical" expectations;

---

[55] http://nonprofit.about.com/
[56] S. Godin, *Permission marketing. Turning Strangers into Friends, and Friends into Customers* (1999).

- *brand value*, that is the brand's value in its own market segment;
- *brand identity*, that is the universe of reference created by the company;
- *brand experience*, that is the brand's regular use, already experienced by the audience;
- *brand activation*, since brand stories are often aimed at involving new customers so that they will change their consuming behaviour;
- *brand franchise*, or the loyalty degree to the brand, which through the audience's response to the new narratives and to the brand stories, will allow the company to differentiate its products.

In order to take an active part in those different aspects of the brand, the "participative consumers" and the brand stories mainly use: the originality of ideas; the presence of *early adopters* potentially able to become the brand's sounding board; the use of at least one character (testimonial) in order to favour the self-identification of the consumer and leading he or she into the story; and the use of mainstream narrative rules and traditional advertising techniques.

Brand stories, however, never represent the main asset of a transmedial promotional campaign, but they are instruments able to make the image and the success of the brand even more innovative. Such a goal recalls the "rhetoric of lovemarks"[57], as it was termed in 2004 by Kevin Roberts to define the fundamental relationship existing between the brand and the consumer's emotional archive, a crucial element for the consumer to be able to interact with all the media involved in a transmedia communicative system[58].

An example?

---

[57] K. Roberts, *Lovemarks. The Future Beyond Brands* (2004).
[58] A. M. Muniz Jr, T.C. O' Guinn, *Brand Community*, in "Journal of Consumer Research" (2001).

In June 2009 Baddy Media created an app-vertising campaign aiming at promoting the Busch Entertaining brand in a cross-platform perspective. Busch Entertaining is a company that operates Sea World and Busch Gardens. A Facebook application, a website and an iPhone app sharing a photo challenge game were created. Users were shown two pictures from one of the company's theme parks and had to identify the difference between them. Along the way, customers could also become fans of the different pages of each of its theme parks. When the game was completed either on the website, the Facebook app, or the iPhone app, the user's score could be sent back to the social network to be shared with friends linked to original stories and shared content[59]... Always remaining in a rewarding space within the boundaries of the brand's imaginative universe of reference.

At other times, on the other hand, the advertising message becomes unbearably aggrandizing, or a brand's image aggressive and conveying a sense of misleading modalities of promotion. Now, since the users/authors of the transmedia generation are particularly sensitive to the aggressive strategies of some brands, as well as being alert towards the mechanisms of communication, the answer lies in projects and narratives aiming at strongly mocking or contrasting the brand, through the smart editorial strategies given by *adbusting* of *subvertising*.

Subvertisers represent a counter-cultural movement which all acts worldwide through forms of advanced interaction and which has as its prime adversary the advertising messages inhabiting the urban spaces, working both on the plane of visual impact and on that of the construction of meaning[60]. There obviously are two ways to do that, one more constructive and the other more destructive. An example?

---

[59] http://blog.thoughtpick.com/
[60] the adbusters movement is headed by Adbusters Media Foundation, a Canadian no profit organization founded in 1989 by Kalle Lasn and Bill Schmalz. http://www.subvertising.org.

For the 2007 campaign *What Would Jesus Buy?*, dedicated to the fight against consumerism and the usual excesses of the Christmas period[61], producer Morgan Spurlock (who made *Super Size Me* in 2004) released a documentary on the extravagant, traveling preaching of an unlikely circuit-rider, Reverend Billy, founder of the Stop Shopping Church. The movie, then out on DVD and diffused as an on-line narrative, was a reminder and an open parody of everything, from graphics to the project's product placement, in the average Disney Christmas movies.

These forms of subvertising and adbusting hardly can be made part of promotion or communication plans, yet they are very effective when it comes to political and cause-related marketing campaigns, for authors of participative transmedial narratives can be found not only among the average user of mainstream narratives, as it is with fanfictions, but also within marginalized subcultures, or among culture jammers[62], as happens in subvertising, constantly fighting against dominant enclaves of the global media flux.

Synergistic Narratives

More recent than participative narratives, twenty years since their first emergence, narratives of the synergistic type[63] have already produced on a global scale a vaster corpus of stories, tales and artistic experiences. They now tend toward hyperproliferation and the saturation of the audience, made by more disorganized authors than the participative and with more infrequent use.

---

[61] http://wwjbmovie.com/

[62] Fora n in-depth on *jammers culture*: G., Branswyn, *Jamming the media: a citizen's guide: reclaiming the tools of communication* (1997).

[63] For *synergistic storytelling in* entertainment and Ivan Askwith's definition: http://dir.salon.com/story/tech/feature/2003/05/12/matrix_universe/index.html

As a matter of fact, in synergistic narratives the tale is created purposefully by the author, and one project is not necessarily connected to the others. These are the features common to all the different forms of collaborative synergistic narratives:

- the *experimental nature* of the tales, always presented as innovative and revolutionary projects;
- the need for industrial processes and clear roles when the narrative is shared between several authors, as well as the necessity of a *final mentorship* for projects;
- the use of rewards and short term deadlines to reach the most efficient outcome;
- the use of editorial systems based on at least one canonical medium (generally the web).

Moreover, with respect to the "imaginative communities"[64] of participative narratives, the synergistic:

- involve the creation by authors who do not know each other, of specific portions and stages of a comprehensive narrative;
- allow authors to mutually alter their own creations;
- are not necessarily connected to pre-existing genres;
- alternatively use professional or amateur authors, never mixing them with each other.

What comes out of all those indicators is that participative narratives represent the most widespread narrative prototype

---

[64] About theoretical definition and the recognition of imaginative communities as consumers groups within narratives: B. Anderson, *Comunità immaginate. Origine e diffusione dei nazionalismi* (1996).

in "narrative marketing" and in the promotion and launch of projects and narratives, while the synergistic are more effective in the planning phase of artistic and interactive narratives.

From the authors' point of view, then, participative narratives are more often used in massive editorial experiences and projects and tend to expand the narrative; those collaborative and synergistic, on the contrary, are more suitable to exclusive projects and experiences and tend to a timely closing of the narration. In this perspective, the three forms of synergistic narrative most used on a world scale are: wikinovels, hyperserial and other forms of polymorphic narrative in entertainment; videogames in advertising; and urban experiences, reality games, urban quest and LARPs in events.

FROM THE WIKI NOVEL TO THE SMS POETRY

The necessary requirements for a huge failure are all there: lack of rules or discipline, an inclination towards juxtaposition, narcissism, inability to bring its way to tell stories into the context of pre-existing narrative frameworks... All risk factors, which could make even the most linear, ordered, and traditional narrative ship wreck in the course of its sail. And that is the case of WikiLit (*wiki literature*). Let us imagine one made of thousands of writers, possibly amateur, without fixed deadlines and with very few editorial limitations.. Who wouldn't be tempted to start up with simpler and shorter narrative forms, in order to limit the possible damage? On the contrary, the most used literary form in synergistic, transmedia projects is that with the most complex structure: the *novel.*

The reason for such a choice must be in the very nature of the novel form itself, from its alexandrine origins to the most original and subversive efforts of contemporary times, already denounced by Michail Bachtin in his essay *Epic and Novel* in which, dealing with the primacy of the novel over other literary genres, he observed how the novel brings in

93

them the issues, the specific semantic incompleteness and, with in contemporary times, the permanently in progress, incomplete contract.[65]

The most open, risky and interactive form, from a transmedia perspective, is thus that of the wiki novel, which contaminates the 19th and 20th Century literary narrative form with the modalities of Wikipedia. The narrative structure of a novel is organised like an encyclopaedic entry; it is created and then updated by a number of theoretically infinite authors, all potentially allowed to modify at any stage the content written before his or her intervention. Moreover, in wiki novels, there is no character, no fixed element which is given to a single narrator. An example? The first wiki novel project in history, *A Million Penguins*, was born out of an idea shared between the British publisher Penguin and the De Montfort University of Leicester, and was active from January to March 2007. At that time a challenge was thrown down on the project's blog with a post named "Rewriting the *Ilyad*." In it, a mysterious John, the publisher's editor, introduced himself, declaring he was the person who was in charge of *how* the novel should be carried on, particularly as concerned plot, characters, dialogue and style: a professional whose task was not to make any edits to the text itself, but who was to follow the development of the story making comments, suggesting small changes, revisions and possible directions to take as the narrative progressed[66]. The project's tight schedule and the precise administration of the platform made it happen: *A Million Penguins* was completed, one of the very few which achieved such a result in publishing all over the world. *A Million Penguins* is therefore an exemplary case of synergistic narrative and of a transmedia project with wider ambitions. A completely different initiative was that launched in 2002 by the British newspaper *The Guardian*, in partnership with the telephone company Orange:

---

[65] M. Bachtin, *Epic and the novel*, in: C. S., Janovi☐ (ed.), *Estetica e romanzo* (1979).
[66] http://thepenguinblog.typepad.com/the_penguin_blog/2007/03/a_million_pengu.html

a competition for poems and content on any subject to be written within the space of the 160 characters of a mobile short text message, which was fairly successful (within a few days about 7500 compositions were sent) and at the same time granted itself a vast media echo-chamber all over the world, even creating a new literary form of expression: *SMS Poetry*. Apart from its length, the use of wiki novel, weblit and all the different forms of interactive literature within synergistic transmedia projects remains even now a limited phenomenon, even thought it *is* an expressive form with high imaginative potential, particularly for its effectiveness in expanding a narrative outside the boundaries of the most traditional channels of a project with a simultaneous, multiplatform distribution.

HYPERSPACE NEEDS HYPERSERIAL

What happens when a synergistic transmedia narrative changes its medium or is developed through different media languages?

Net-drama, for instance, appears on the Internet in 2004 as a narrative form in between theatre and net-art. A dramaturgical, experimental product that landed on the Net, it kept its hybrid nature, parcelling out its content between literature, radio and cinema. For this reason it ended up being a little rigid and not suitable to the existing transmedial communicative systems: it soon disappeared. An example?

Secret Room, a 2004 Italian-Australian production, is noteworthy for being among the first net-dramas in Net history. Its narrative device involved ten people gathering every night for dinner in one of the characters' houses, to chat and tell each other stories and share experiences. Then, at some stage, something happened: the dinner and the scene stopped and the audience was brought into a (online) secret chamber where thousands of windows started to open; to the user those windows were unmanageable. During the theatre performance, meanwhile, the group filmed everything that happened and split this material into short fragments, adding to them brand new animations – 45 tracks in all – and sending each movie to a different HTML page. The novelty existed in the fact that the director was neither the programmer, nor the user: the pages were in fact randomly refreshed by the computer each time, both in terms of length and in terms of sequence. The whole mechanism was then multiplied through a series of *pop ups* littering the screen and suggesting to the user alternative cuts and paths to take through the labyrinth. There was actually one single way on 45 to gain access to the secret chamber, an actual website where all the secrets would be eventually revealed, thus closing the narrative device based on the public's surprise endurance.

Following its early disappearance from the web, the term 'net drama' has become sporadic with the passing of time and has been replaced with *hyperserial.* The impromptu narrative forms were advanced at the same time by interactive and serial stories which, in the passage from the audiovisual to the online narrative form, fragment their plots and allow the public to reconstruct them as if they were actual transmedial jigsaws. An example?

After having filmed ,in his own Tampere cellar, dozens of episodes of the hyperserial *Star Wreck: In the Pirkinning*, a parody of *Star Trek*, "the first science fiction serial ever set in Finland", Samulii Torssonen and Timo Vuorensuola left their more then 300 collaborators behind, with their cameras, laptops, weird uniforms and pointed ears[67] to radically change their narrative modalities and forms. Thanks to the amazing success that diffusion by word of web mouth has granted them, they now own a dedicated editorial platform (Star Wreck Studios) and Universal Pictures bought the old *Star Wreck* and produced their second movie, *Iron Sky*, a satirical

---

[67] *Star Wreck* (http://www.starwreck.com/) e *Iron Sky* (http://www.ironsky.net /site/).

alternate history where the Nazis, who escaped to the moon in 1945, are making their return to Earth in 2018, armed to the teeth. Yet this is a model which, over time, has limited the audience, rather than open its narratives to the authors or the transmedia generation; in this view it does represent a step back which leaves narratives by the roadside and it is certainly not looking ahead to the future of contemporary narratives.

If compared to net-drama and to the first experiments of meta-fiction, today's hyperserial must use narrative models closer to those narratives based upon moving experiences, on games and on TV *microfiction*[68]. This is the reason why in the most successful products:

- the format of the episodes is flexible and variable;
- the maximum number of characters speaking at the same time on a single scene is limited;
- the rhythm of each episode is fast, and so it is with the lines spoken by the actors;
- sets and locations alternate, from fixed (with characters) to computer generated (without characters);
- there is no explicit reference (except for occasional incidents) to facts and events from the news; this is to avoid the early outdating of the narrative;
- subcultures and tribes are often portrayed on screen in a more insisted fashion than with more traditional narratives;
- spaces are reserved to the audiences' creativity, even though they may be planned for the following editions of the project;
- extreme care is dedicated to graphics and visual effects, to affect the memorization process of the audience.

---

[68] Definite *minifiction, filler, fiction interstiziali* o *strisce brevi*: le microfiction televisive sono serie lunghe composte da episodi brevi, generalmente di registro comico o sentimentale, legati tra loro senza soluzione di continuità.

An example? Two years after its project *Voyeur*, the U.S. broadcaster HBO came up in September 2009 with a new narrative experiment called *Imagine*. New York, Philadelphia and Washington hosted, with no previous notice or announcement, in sequence, the installation of a huge black cube on whose sides the images of an innovative hyperserial were projected; it was possible to enjoy it in a different way according to the angle one was watching it from. At the same time, online, according to a clear omnivorous system, the official website of the project (www.hboimagine.com) allowed users to enjoy the very same interactive experience by spinning – in a 3D menu – the same cube and changing the point of view of the narrative.

This time in the form of a 41 pieces *puzzle game*, content including video, audio files, letters and images connected to each other, an interactive story and game-like experience that deepens the more one explores it, realized by the BBDO NY agency and released online by The Barbarian Group.

POLYMORPHIC NARRATIVES

An even more interactive form of audiovisual and multiplatform narrative than hyperserial and interactive fiction is the *polymorphic narrative*, made of narratives which make simultaneous use of different media, which can be adapted in progress according to the audience's choices (following trends I have already dealt with when I wrote about the *Doppler effect* on transmedia projects). The main aim of polymorphic narratives is that of allowing its authors/users to *make a unique experience* and totally yield to a flow of stories, adventures and fascinations, a stream whose result is strongly cooperative and emotional. In other words, literature and fiction getting closer to games, with narrative time synchronized to that of performance.

An example? In October 2007 the TV serial *CSI-NY* "landed" in the metaworld of *Second Life*, with a very peculiar idea. In the television narrative, an episode of the series saw protagonist Mac Taylor (Gary Sinise) entering *Second Life* to flush out a murderer who was luring his victims in by surfing the metaworld. Simultaneous to the airing of the episode the authors proposed to the audience three different forms of synergistic performance:

- solve the case through interaction with links on the CBS website, or visiting the *CSI* lab in one of the New York skyscrapers reconstructed within the metaworld of *Second Life* ;
- join in the game *Murder by Zuiker*, following the traces left by the killer in the form of virtual gadgets for the 100 contestants who would get closer to the solution of the case;
- become detective, using the kit for investigations and wearing a uniform, with the possibility of questioning suspects so as to be able to solve the same case which was being aired, built to close with a cliff-hanger and leave the audience hanging ... until the following February!

A complex initiative, then, which added the recreational dimension typical of the treasure hunt or the book game to the television narrative, and at the same time was metaphorically unlocking the doors of the writing section of a great TV series to the narrative model of interactive fiction to the transcoding of narratives and to the additive comprehension[69] typical of the new transmedia narratives.

---

[69] The definition of the audience's additive comprehension in transmedial narratives is due to Neil Young, former Electronic Arts, as it reads in: H. Jenkins, *Convergence... cit.*

Even though for a short fraction of time, when author and user draw close as they do in polymorphic narrative, we are witness to a case of *omusia*, identity, as is more commonly in the case of Alternate Reality Stories. Another form of polymorphic narrative, *ARS* are the result of a contamination between alternate reality games and interactive storytelling and owe their terming to Jane McGonigal, who defines them as interactive performances played online and in real places at the same time, in the space of weeks or months, by small groups, as well as by thousands of participants, committed to a narrative product. An example?

I know people who, some nights, even in the form of avatar, change their features to make them look like those of Jennifer Anniston, Courtney Cox or David Schwimmer, buy wholesale clothes in some simulation and go down into the dusty hull of a galleon harboured on the shores of Caribbean Breezes Island, in *Second Life*'s Metaverse. In the days before they created the scripts, scheduled the scenes and decided all the movements their avatars would make, some of them had modified a location in order to make it similar to the famous greenish Greenwich Village apartment, while others had decided the camera movements (with respective angles, lighting, point of view, framing) and the musical score until, one day, eventually it was all ready for "shooting". It is then time to set a rendezvous with the public, that is to say other avatars, to observe the narrative directly "on the spot", or interfere with it, suggesting gags, situations, *escamotages*, while the narrative itself is in progress.

Whether the aim is to recreate an episode of the series *Friends* or produce an original sitcom, from the point of view of techniques used for the production of the narrative there is no basic difference: alternate reality stories are actual *machinima*[70], that is to say they use actors, locations, and a 3D

---

[70] Short form for *machine cinema* or *machine animation* using real time footage through the use od 3D graphic motors from virtual games and worlds. Created in 1996 with a video

graphics engine from a virtual universe or videogame and then place them inside their own original, strictly user-generated stories.

In the above mentioned example about *Friends*, backgrounds and avatars come from *Second Life* (for this reason the more specific and branded definition of *Second Stories*), but the question is: what kind of contribution can these narrative forms give to a transmedia project? Being totally transversal narrative forms, alternate reality stories use the traditional genres of literary narrative, film grammar, the dramaturgical structure of TV serials and the interactivity of videogames mostly to create new active spaces for audiences within more traditional transmedia projects, in the course of the narrative and after its ending. Some examples?

In May 2008 the first live musical from the metaworld was produced: *Second Life Odissea* – The Musical, a remake of Homer's poem with dozens of avatars actively singing, dancing and acting in front of an audience made of hundreds of skins sitting in a Greek amphitheatre; the purpose was to raise funds for the African Medical Research Foundation.

In literature, moreover, a very personal example comes from the first Italian *machinima* set in *Second Life* for the promotion of a novel I wrote in 2008: *All'immobilità qualcosa sfugge (To Stillness Something Slips Away)*. This is a choral story, based on the use of multilinear dramaturgies, telling about three couples violently imploding on one another in the space of one single night, during which the protagonists would use their avatars to meet and cheat on their partners, in *Second Life*[71]. From narrative to game, in this case, as it was for that of *CSI*, the idea agreed with the publisher was to create an alternate ending of the novel and two virtual stages in *Second*

---

exploiting the videogame's Quake graphic motor, machinimas are today an actual expressive form with a n institutional portal (http://machinima.com) and an official festival organized by the Academy of Machinima Arts & Sciences (http://festival.machinima.org/).

[71] M. Giovagnoli, *All'immobilità qualcosa sfugge* (2008).

Life and, finally, a contest for machinima and *songvid* realized by the readers and inspired by the story. Not simple book trailers, but "narratives within narratives" to be shown during the live appearances in the launching tour of the novel and in a viral online campaign on social networks and online broadcasters with the aim of giving the most creative part of the audience filterless, immediate visibility.

Anyhow, before leaving alternate reality stories behind, even though comprehensive coverage of the topic would require greater autonomy, it is convenient to at least hint at the form of synergistic narrative *par excellence*, that is to say MMoRPGs, which are extremely autonomous in their nature but do not often involve transmedia forms of contamination in their imaginative universes. Still it would be sufficient to quickly browse the names of the most famous games in recent years, from *Final Fantasy* to *World of Warcraft*, from *Lord of the Rings Online* to *Star Wars Galaxies* and *City of Heroes*, to realize how MMoRPGs are playing a most crucial role in the creation and the management of the imaginary in our entertainment. MMoRPGs allow users, in other words, to inhabit and play with the imaginary universes other media create, and do so with excellent competitive devices.

Originally an electronic evolution of war simulators and table games, from 5th Century Hindu *Chaturanga* to early 19th century Prussian *Kriegsspiel*, as well as of contemporary role-playing games (from Dave Arneson's and Gary Gygax's 1972 *Dungeons & Dragons* on), MMoRPGs started their adventure in 1996-97, creating digital *othernesses* where it would be possible to exalt Pierre Levy's four variables necessary to develop collective intelligence[72]: *nomadic mobility* (of players and characters played by them), *control over territory, ownership over commodities* (exchanged both in the virtual and in the real world), and *mastery over knowledge* (either shared or hidden, according to the objectives of the games). Compared to other

---

[72] P. Lévy, *L'intelligence...* cit.

typologies of transmedia narratives, MMoRPGs stand out for the use of open narratives, which can at any stage be influenced by users-narrators and for the possibility of altering through the game the experience and the representation of the "real" as it is lived both collectively and individually[73]. The narrative becomes thus interactive and inter-operative at the same time and the author's intervention consists in the creating adventures (*quests*) and testing skills (*tricks*), all enjoyable "in private" or "in groups" connected via server. In MMoRPGs, then, the narrative rhythm is not preset and the stories are set in fictional universes, arranged in islands (primary, secondary, and so on…) but then made more chaotic by the users' actions.

The user plays and tells the story together with the other players using different options for their perspective. Sociality among players can be either peaceful or antagonistic, is organized in groups (guilds, factions, and so on…) or in systems of alliances created by the users. As it is with adbusting, then, MMoRPG can also display its community of subverters, in fact: the *modders*, users who can alter a game's source code "from ground level", either by personalizing it, or by inserting elements which are not real in the model created by its developers. An editorial practice – modding – which is now also a marketing technique, as it was for instance the case of the launch of *Grand Theft Auto: Vice City* in 2004, when modders gave the antagonists of the game an XJ8 Jaguar which was not in the corporate plans. The only element, which does remain the same within the game, is the form of internal learning provided for by the narrative; it can be considered as an *expert paradigm* (EP) crucial to the success of the narrative. It is exactly because of the presence of stirring, user-friendly expert paradigms that, with their immersive presence on the Internet, MMoRPGs could gradually gain spaces in other

[73] T., Flew, *New Media: an introduction* (2008).

media, hybridizing with and contaminating comics, cartoons and movies all over the world. An example?

In 2008 French Studio Ankama created the MMoRPG *Wakfu*, a tactical, fantasy role-playing game one could play online with 14 different classes of characters. Even to the producers themselves such a structure appeared too rich and ambitious, although in a few months *Wakfu*'s unexpected success allowed the game to become an animated series and a comics series too, as had happened before with *Dofus*, also produced by Ankama. It was distributed all over Europe and is today one of the best moneymaking transmedial franchises of the Old Continent.

CODE NAME: ADVERGAME

There are forms of hybrid transmedial narratives which today move on the wire hung on the border between videogames and advertising, born out of the following realization: a significant part of the public today gets fond of a given brand in a more long-lasting and effective way than before, and it prefers to "play" the brand, rather than just listen to its slogans. Yet advergames are an independent product, albeit insufficient if considered within transmedial products; they mainly work as an entertaining asset of promotional campaigns based on omnivorous communicative systems, essentially aiming at the pathemic involvement of the consumer.

The first advergame in history is considered that created by Dan Ferguson and Mike Bielinski, of Blockdot, in 1998: a goliardic game sent by e-mail to an undefined group of addresses and inspired by the adventures of Bill Clinton and Monica Lewinsky and associated, a few days later, with the advertising campaign of a famous American brand. Interactivity and the consumer/user's freedom of choice represent advergames' dramaturgical basis. Moreover, unlike the majority of transmedia narratives, advergames do not openly declare in advance the *regles du jeu*, but aim at, on the other hand, the self-training and self-satisfaction experienced by the player. The most ideal means they use is certainly the web, which is more and more integrated with free apps for smartphones. Besides, as a form of narrative strictly connected to commercial products and services, advergames can offer transmedia promotion campaigns:

- informal and spontaneous, positive memorization (*mark up*) of the brand, granted by the positive interaction given by the experience of gaming;
- a longer *company time* experienced between consumer and product, thanks to the game;
- development of a different *brand awareness* by the consumer/player about the brand's universe (for example with experience and educational games);
- the creation of a database of consumers which would be impossible to reach out in any other way, and who are – on the contrary – very present in the advergame microcosm.

The most credited classification in advergames is that made in 2001 by Jane Chen and Mattew Ringel, of the New York agency KPE, which made a distinction between *associative*, *illustrative* and *demonstrative* advergames.

In associative advergames the brand is displayed during the course of the game. In illustrative advergames the brand is interpreted and integrated within the devices of the game. Finally, in demonstrative advergames, the brand is directly tested and experienced by the consumer during the game.

In associative advergames the communication axis is completely overbalanced on the message, reducing the narration to a simple paradigm or pattern, in favor of the game's emotional revenue. An example?

In 2008 a partnership between Italian motorcycle company Ducati and power company Enel generated an online magazine which displayed, together with news and contests dedicated to its community, a simulation advergame played online. At the end of the race, the player could "migrate" on the *Second Life* company's sim or in the Ducati blog, for the prize-giving ceremony. This process, however, would not involve any form of creative contribution to the creation or to the development of the narrative by the player/consumer.

A higher narrative degree can be observed in illustrative advergames, where the brand can identify: the *location* where the adventure takes place, the *protagonist* of the story or the *objective* to be achieved in the game. In the 2002 advergame *Flip the Mix* by M&M's, for instance, the objective of the game was to line up chocolate sweets in order to complete the different levels of the game and win product prizes: "from the brand, with the brand, for the brand", what David Marshall calls intertextual commodity in transmedia narratives. A productive other than editorial approach: in the brand's communicative project, in fact, it is possible to find an integration between entertainment and marketing content, leading the consumer from a traditional medium on to a digital one, and vice-versa[74].

A further degree of participation is moreover distinctive of demonstrative advergames, in which the consumer can alternatively:

- directly influence the narrative structure, stepping in the brand's shoes, as in, for instance, the 2005 Siemens advergame *Buildy Game*, where the player plays the role of the manager of one of the major projects implemented by the corporation all over the world (involving the construction of stadiums, airports,

---

[74] D. Marshall, *The New Intertextual Commodity*, in: D. Harris (ed.), *The Book of New Media* (2002).

hospital wards and so on...), thus obtaining information about those Siemens products which are most suitable to each scenario (it also involved a prize competition);

- directly experience the brand through the game, as it is for instance with the advergame Vince *Carter* produced by Nike, where the player wears the basketball champ's uniform, independently interpreting the game and testing different models of sneakers in an involving dunk shot tournament.

The synergistic dimension of the narrative in advergames, if compared to other transmedia forms, is always managed by the user and is not connected to the live modality which can be found in other media of the communicative system. Despite this, the future of advertising is in its hands, as well as a more and more interactive and pathemic modality of promotion.

URBAN EXPERIENCES & REALITY GAMES

Reality narratives are stories lived by their authors, by the public and by the characters of the tale, physically and digitally at the same time. Whether it's small groups of users acting inside an urban circuit or hundreds of actors in costume, all gathered on the top of a hill or among the castles' merlons, in reality narratives the new media integrate and enrich the human sensorial experience, providing new forms of awareness and consumption. More than moving experience and expanding environment narratives, they offer the audience new territories for an active reflection, a confrontation, a content performance and competition.

The most frequented and better-established reality narratives of the last decade in terms of transnational projects are: *urban quests*, *urban experiences* and *LARPs*. These narrative forms are very different both in what concerns the editorial and narrative perspective, and in terms of user spaces offered to the public, from the more traditional to the new media environments.

Although reality narratives can offer marketing and advertising deeper narrative dimensions, in fact, based on perception rather than on appearance, it is nevertheless in the cultural and touristic valorization of local products and traditions that their own aggregative and explorative nature appears more effective through transmedia communication systems.

An example? Let's start right from commercial urban quests and go back in time to 2007, when there were three hundred people who came to the perforated stage. White overalls and work-suits, in this Italian summer which takes no prisoners: Milan, Rome, and Naples. They are all ready. Some are sitting on the sidewalk, others gathered in small circles frantically typing letters and numbers on their palm computers and next-generation mobile phones. They may look like survivors of a city marathon, but they are actually the selected winners of *Navigator Hunt*, the first great Italian urban quest realized on a non-existing city circuit, a virtual otherness coming out of the hybridization of three different urban fabrics, implemented by the Nokia media company in cooperation with environmental agency Legambiente. A middle step between the pure adventure narrative and a cause related marketing experience, the project's payoff is very clear, after all: "Have you ever explored three cities at the same time?" and so the campaign teaser appears to be:

> Milan, Rome, Naples are joined together in Italy's greatest treasure hunt. 60 teams, 300 players in the finals. From September 16th to October 13, 2007. You can win dozens of Nokia 6110 Navigator and the newest Renault Twingo Nokia.

In this case, as always happens in reality narratives, the narrative has a two-goal structure basis: where the audience's final achievement shall be, or the end of the game (in other cases the urban fabric is real and the goal of the game is simply to completely cover the path), and the valorization of the subject (learning to respect the environment consciously moving inside the city fabrics).

From the perspective of the construction and management of the narrative, urban quests are a hybrid form of reality narrative, hovering between life-size games and gamebooks, and, within its narrative, join into a relationship the territory (seen as a network), the citizen (seen as an active consumer) and the city (seen as a social network). There are instances of team adventures being posthumously collected into tales and stories, when the experience is over, mostly in the form of an online diary, but that is not the rule. The typical dimension of those kinds of narratives is mainly real time.

A literary and educational variation of urban quests, mostly devoted to "genre fiction" and to the classics, is represented by *Google Lit Trips* (or Google Literature Trips), virtual journeys and treasure hunts played by groups and teams (of mainly students) which perform actions modifying the geographical and cultural imagery of a given story, entrusting the reader with the experience of a "second grade narrative" run through the use of an online localizer provided by Google Maps, as well as software dedicated to the creation of presentations, slideshows and multimedia animations (in a concrete, user generated perspective).

Architectural, artistic and socio-anthropological variation of these narrative forms, finally, are represented by *urban experiences*, which transform cities reconstructed in living tissues by geoblog, integrating life and culture experiences with multimedia content accessible via smartphone, with QR code or radiowalk along emotional paths structured in wider "networks of signified". An example?

In 2011, an original *walkshow* was organized focusing on the theme "Socially Responsible Media" with an emotional journey through pagan Rome, with an itinerary symbolically starting from the "Bocca della Verità" (representing human instinct), to get to the Roman Forum (law), via Rome's ghetto (struggle for equality), the Capitol (new institutions) and the Colosseum (the media-arena, the *ludus*). The different stages of the journey were animated with sounds, 3D animations, short documentaries, and written accounts.

Finally, based on a closer relationship between non-specialized media, traditional forms of narrative and entertainment, we have *reality games*, a richer, more interactive version of TV reality shows where authors/consumers do not recreate emulation, but self-recognition with the protagonists of the narrative which is developing online in front of their own eyes.

In this sense it can be a valid example to mention the case of *8 in Punto* (*Eight o'clock sharp*), created by the car company FIAT in October 2008. A webserial and a reality game divided into episodes following the on-the-road adventures of eight competitors, four men and four women, divided into two teams driving two cars and broadcast in real time. Eight weeks and four big cities (Milan, Boulogne, Florence and Rome) made the narrative arena of the game, "driven" from the beginning by the users through suggestions and comments published on social media and with occasional presence of stars and guests within the tale.

A last form of reality narrative is that, a middle way, which stands between urban quests and reality games: the LARP (*Live Action Role Playing*). "Costume" performances involving the online and live participation of groups of users, it has similar modalities to those of role playing and narrative games. Objective: re-enacting — both physically and digitally — of ancient battles or social-cultural events, never associable to commercial brands and, in this case too, often filmed and broadcast online after the event. Mostly operative in no-profit areas or in solidarity projects, or for the valorization of tourism or the environment, LARPs originated most probably with the group "Dagorhir Outdoor Improvisational Battle

Games" founded in 1977 in Washington, after the role play game *Dungeons and Dragons*. LARPs use stories and plots created for everybody by a larpwright – the equivalent to a Game Master of role-play games, only more skilled in terms of choreography, localization, theatre direction and improvisation. A LARP's narrative time can vary from a few hours to some days, seamlessly. The intervention of media has generally very limited interactive boundaries and can be considered an active party in a narrative or an exclusive witness to the performance. Its rhythm depends on the plot, as much as on the movements of the actors on the field. Stories represent a collection ranging from committed, avant-guard narratives (*arthaus*), to theatre and spectacular narratives (like *freeforms*, with fights taking place within fests, re-enacting historical battles). Moreover, as in the case of fanfictions, while the narrative is in progress, the protagonists can interpret real life characters (*in character*) or fictional characters (*out of character*).

Frequently used in conventions and theme parks, the high value of reality narratives in terms of experiences is a witness of the crucial role played, in transmedia narratives, by the confrontation between history and everyday life, real territories and digital landscapes, reportage narratives and fictional narratives, but, more importantly, between the human being and active space, beyond the artistic or commercial purpose of an editorial project.

CHAPTER FIVE

Fancy... a Paradigm?

Even if considering the three-act structure of the story that dates back to Aristotle's *Poetics*, organized in:

SET UP > CONFRONTATION > RESOLUTION

transmedia tales and projects use several storytelling paradigms that vary greatly from each other, both if they have a single author and if they are the result of participative or synergistic involvement of the audience. To carry out projects and works simultaneously distributed on multiple media, creators and transmedia producers use narrative bibles, interactive maps, flow charts and protocols that are re-workings and crossbred works from other narrative disciplines: for instance, screenplays, game designs and information architectures.

Thus, everyone creates his own paradigm over time, but must define "dramaturgic outlines" that are useful for entertainment, advertising and information as well as for institutional communication or tourism, in the artistic field or the educational one...

Considering the basic structure of this reasoning about transmedia storytelling, I will analyze the three storytelling paradigms most in use today. They are: the *transformational arc of the character, the hero's journey and the twelve stations structure*[75].

It has to be said from the start that the most important discriminating factor of using a particular dramaturgic model is its *function*: as the three paradigms have different features, their applicability differs in cases of a single medium or in multiple assets of a communicative system.

The Transformational Arc of the Character

In order to describe the inner development process of the main character of a transmedia story, the author must equally distribute hints in the multiple media involved and attentively tell autonomous stories that, at the same time, must be stimulating and able to create, in their respective audiences, as *spontaneous* a process of sharing and cooperation as possible. Thus, what does the transformational arc of a character involve, concretely? And what is its relation and use in the field of transmedia narratives?

The paradigm of the transformational arc of the character was created in 2007 by the American editor Dara Marks, and is itself an evolution of Syd Field's development of the Aristotelic three-act structure, with three different levels of reading which are:

- the plot of the story, interpreted through the events (obstacles, further problems, strokes of luck...) that are experienced by the character;

---

[75] L. Forlai, A. Bruni, *Come raccontare una grande storia che appassioni il pubblico* (1996).

- the primary subplot of the story, which consists of the relations (intentionally or unintentionally) created by the character (love, hate, friendship…);
- the secondary subplot of the story, which is the process of inner (positive or negative) transformation of the character.[76]

Considering this pattern, the perfect narrative structure lets the three dramaturgic dimensions of the character develop following the story, in a communicative system of one or more media. Starting with the *set-up* of the tale, passing through the *first turning point* until the *midpoint* to the *second turning point* and then the *climax* and the *resolution* of the tale, the character will develop from an initial status of *resistance* to the inner transformation, until a *release* that will change him forever.

Img. 2 - The *Transformational arc of the character* paradigm.

Moreover, considering this paradigm, the *resistance* process of a character follows a process that starts from a *fatal flaw* (an essential lacking quality, fatal mistake or unbearable condition) in the beginning, and goes through an *awakening* (the character

---

[76] D. Marks, *Inside Story. The Power of the Transformational Arc* (2007).

is not completely aware of a new situation created by an unexpected event) until the first turning point of the tale, and then through an *enlightenment* (a complete awareness of the inner conflict) in the *midpoint* of the story. Then, the *release* process through which the character faces, matures and accepts his own transformational arc, allows him to pass from the midpoint to the second turning point of the tale, proceeding from a status of *grace* towards a *fall*. Following this fall, he arrives to face death at the climax of the story. This is the point in which the *transformational moment* of the character starts, and it finishes his transformational arc.

All these passages, in most of cases, are developed through a mainstream narrative, but in the transmedia tales they inevitably have to be "gradually" shared with the audiences throughout the development of the tale.

An example? Between 1982 and 1985, on the English magazine "*Warrior*" there was a weekly strip publication of *V for Vendetta*, a tale written by Alan Moore and illustrated by David Lloyd. A few years later, the several publications of this comic were collected in a *graphic novel* which, in 2005, was released as a movie directed by James McTeigue, based on a screenplay by Andy and Larry Wachowski.

Comics, novels and movies all accurately reproduce the tale: an uchrony within a post-nuclear setting, in a future ruled by an Orwellian and obscure fascist regime (as in *1984*) with catastrophic corruptions drawn from Ray Bradbury (*Fahrenheit 451*).

In the story, the plot, primary and secondary subplots are focused on the protagonist V, who survived a terrible concentration camp and is now determined to take revenge by killing his jailors. Meanwhile, (through the use of a clear *two goal structure*), he arranges a "final" attack on the offices of the regime (*plot*). But one night, V meets the young Evey, a lonely young lady marginalized as he is, with whom he becomes infatuated; she will stand by him until the end of the tale (primary subplot). Moreover, thanks to her, when V dies, his desire for justice spreads to the whole population: by putting on his mask – the one which belonged to Guy Fawkes, an antimonarchic conspirator who, in 1605, planned the bombing of the English Parliament – the population will finally begin to fight against the regime (secondary subplot).

All the stages of the pattern of V's character transformational arc can be found both in the graphic novel and in the movie, from resistance to the awakening, from the status of grace to the final climax and resolution of the tale. However, in contrast to the graphic novel, in the movie: imprisonment and all the other processes of existential friction are only slightly mentioned, while the imprisonment he imposes on the young girl, to make her follow his passage from life to death, seems to be more violent and detailed.

However, even with some internal variations, the paradigm of the transformational arc in *V for Vendetta* was used again for the launch of the movie, for the advertising campaign of the book (on paper press magazines, on Web…), in the novel by Steve Moore[77] based on the movie's script and in its theater adaptations (for example, the one on stage in Sweden in 2006); they all confirm the tale as a symbolic example of transmedia narrative focused on the transformational arc of the protagonist, ready to be re-created by the *emergent communities of knowledge* organized in fandoms and in communities of an even more tactical, temporary and intentional kind.

The "Transmedia Hero's Journey"

The "Hero's journey" paradigm is rooted in studies about the creation of myths in the folk tale and oral tradition genres,

---

[77] S. Moore, *V for Vendetta* (2006).

from Vladimir J. Propp's *Morphology of the Folktale* to the Jungian Hero Archetype's theorization, and then from Joseph Campbell's studies and his *Hero with a Thousand Faces* to the TV screenplay by Chris Vogler[78]. Referring to the Structuralist lesson applied to folklore and epic tales, the "Hero's Journey" lets the structure of the plot and the story of the tale depend on the mythological experience of its protagonist.

From the point of view of transmedia narratives and projects, the Hero's journey paradigm is the most effective for supportive communicative systems, but it often offers a low level of interaction with the audience. The media to which it refers are cinema and games: the audience likes to identify, in particular, with the hero on the big screen or "play the hero" online, by mobile phone or console. All the bridges identified from one medium to another throughout the tale have this same basic expectation. Surely, in transmedia tales and projects, for multiple media and multiple audiences, sometimes there would be multiple "hero's journeys", which are developed in an autonomous or participative way by the audience; but the interaction never reaches a high level. Considering the analysis of this paradigm, the twelve steps of the journey are:

1. *The Ordinary World*: the hero is introduced to the audience living in his world at the beginning of the tale. In transmedia tales, this bridge very often uses an external narrator, omniscient or even invisible, as happens, for example, during the entry of the competitors in a reality show's arena.

2. *The Call to Adventure*: suddenly, something shakes up the hero's life, or "The hero starts off in a mundane situation of normality from which some information is received that acts

---

[78] To refer to the creation of the "Hero's journey" narrative paradigm: C. Vogler, *The Writer's Journey* (2007) and J. Campbell, *The Hero with a Thousand Faces* (1949) and C.G. Jung, *Gli archetipi dell'inconscio collettivo* (1968).

as a call to head off into the unknown"[79]. In the transmedia tale, this "interruption" of the story's flow is a topical moment, which has to be used in the main medium of the project, but then repeated in the other media in order to reinforce the uniqueness of the hero's experience. It could happen, for example, in the game intro of a videogame taken from a movie.

3. *Refusal of the Call*: the hero tries to turn away from the adventure, but can't do it. In front of a "call", some of the characters act on impulse[80], accepting the challenge; others, instead, totter and are reluctant. "Refusal of the summons converts the adventure into its negative. Walled in boredom, hard work, or 'culture,' the subject loses the power of significant affirmative action and becomes a victim to be saved. His flowering world becomes a wasteland of dry stones and his life feels meaningless—even though, like King Minos, he may through titanic effort succeed in building an empire or renown. Whatever house he builds, it will be a house of death: a labyrinth of cyclopean walls to hide from him his minotaur. All he can do is create new problems for himself and await the gradual approach of his disintegration."[81] In transmedia tales, if spaces of real-time interaction with the audience of one or more media exist, in the moment of the hero's refusal, it is always better to let the audience act, in order to allow them to empathize more directly with their new favorite character.

4. *Meeting with the Mentor*: the hero meets someone who gives him training, advice and suggestions that will help him in the journey and in his life. The mentor is the Jungian archetype and a "guide" incarnation. "More often than not, this supernatural mentor will present the hero with one or more talismans or artifacts that will aid them later in their quest." In transmedia projects, moreover, he addresses both

---

[79] http://en.wikipedia.org/wiki/Monomyth
[80] Vladimir J. Propp defines this kind of heroes as *seekers*, in: V. J. Propp, *Morphology of the Folktale* (1968).
[81] J. Campbell, *The Hero with a Thousand Faces* (1949).

the Hero and the audience simultaneously, and each time his voice challenges or helps the user to correctly interpret the experience of the tale.

5. *Crossing the Threshold*: at the end of Act One, the hero leaves the Ordinary World and enters the special, unknown world of his journey. In transmedia tales, the first threshold is always presented in each medium of the publishing project and it is the first, real and basic moment to make the audiences of multiple media collaborate among them.

6. *Tests, Allies and Enemies*: once the threshold is crossed, the Hero and his audiences (with their allies and against their enemies) start their experiences and face challenges from one medium to another. To let himself be involved and immersed, the user must earn a good score, reaching visibility or power exactly when, in the tale, a choice or action is made or started.

7. *Approach to the in-Most Cave*: the hero and his allies prepare for the major challenge in the Special World. In order to positively reflect the emotions the protagonist has had, it is necessary that each of the involved media interpret the emotional tension of the character in its own way.

8. *The Ordeal*: the hero enters a central space in the Special World and faces his greatest fear[82]. In transmedia tales, this is the most important moment for the live use of the tale; when it ends, the audiences or communities, in particular those in new media, will begin to ask themselves the same question, "Will he succeed?", as we saw, for example, in *CSI* in *Second Life*.

9. *The Reward*: the Hero gains something special by facing death ...and the audiences too! For example, by using personal *gifts* or special content addressed to the main followers of the project and to the main champions of the tale (again, using social network campaigns or community activism as well as mobile narratives and little events).

---

[82]http://en.wikipedia.org/wiki/The_Writer's_Journey:_Mythic_Structure_for_Writers

10.   *The Road Back*: the hero leaves the Special World and his adventure, and brings the treasure home. In transmedia tales, this is the point to remind the audience of the best and most emotional moments of the story, at least in one of the multiple media involved, through single videos or trailers, preferably on the web, due to the ease of uploading them and giving audiences access to the content.

11.   *The Resurrection*: the last sacrifice, the last climax, the last death and rebirth of the Hero, to bring about a change in the inhabitants of his own Ordinary World and in the audience. In transmedia tales, a narrative strategy often used at this point is to develop the tale in two directions simultaneously. For example, during a TV series broadcast, on one side there will be the generalist media focused, firstly, on the protagonist, and then on the other characters; on the other side, on the Internet and in the content created for mobile users, there is the opposite process, focusing on the secondary characters (maybe to develop into a new series), then focusing on the protagonist of the tale.

12.   *Return with the Elixir*: "the hero returns home or continues the journey, bearing some element of the treasure that has the power to transform the world as the hero has been transformed". But first, something (the elixir) made him and his story immortal. What? In transmedia tales, this is the moment to spur into action, for the last time, all the audiences of the project; it might be through a final contest, which would be able to have them converge on a single, final arena of the tale, as often happens in the charity or fund-raising projects.

Img. 3 - The *Hero's Journey* paradigm.

The epic tone and the strong imaginative power of the protagonist of the tale make the "hero's journey" paradigm one of the most used patterns in transmedia storytelling. But the presence of numerous archetypes (heroes, shadows, mentors, herald, threshold guardians, shapeshifters, tricksters and allies) allows the audience to side temporarily with other characters throughout the tale. This helps the sharing of the imaginative universe of the story and, at the same time, works very well in the "marketing of the tale" of the transmedia culture. An example?

The *24* TV-series, which due to its *framed*-narrative structure combines the narrative pattern of a TV reality game with that of traditional fiction. In fact, in *24,* each season tells about a sequence of events that take place during a single day, through 24 episodes of 45 minutes each – which last 60 minutes after considering the advertising breaks – and each lasting for an hour of real time in the fiction. By using *frame narratives,* that is the division of the pattern into sub-frames (technically, *split-screens*), the audience simultaneously follows different narrative levels and stories developed through multiple subplots. But this is not the end of the process. Throughout the years, the series has expanded into different

121

media, specifically videogames, mobile episodes, "webisodes", books, mobile games and comics, but all together followed the same narrative pattern: the hero's journey of the protagonist Jack Bauer, an agent of the Counter Terrorist Unit of Los Angeles, who through the different seasons of the tale and the multiple media of the communicative system of the project has gone from the west coast of the U.S. to Washington, to finally arrive among the skyscrapers of Manhattan.

The "Twelve Stations" Paradigm

The *Twelve Stations Paradigm* is similar to that of the hero's journey, but it is more focused on the character's inner psychology and motivations, dividing the narrative universe into two main spheres of influence opposed to one another: good and bad, right and wrong, protagonist and antagonist, all with their own points of view... It is exactly for this reason that such a model can be applied to mostly competitive transmedia systems, where the single media have the possibility of choosing what side to be on and divide audience between them, often promoting in their own mechanisms participative narrative forms.

The "Twelve Stations" is the outcome of the integration between the model of the Hero's Journey and that of Syd Field and Linda Seger, made by Italian editors Luigi Forlai and Augusto Bruni. It proves very effective in transmedia narrative, especially in that distributed on the web (weblit, fanfictions) – where there is much more opportunity for audience interaction – and in advertising (including in its gaming dimension), where there is a stronger contrast between the characters' motivations and those of the brand and the audience. The twelve stations of the paradigm's structure are:

1. *The Inner Ghost*: an event from the past still haunts the protagonist of the tale. The ghost represents the actual motivation of the character and leads the narrator into using a particular register (strict? Ironic? Subtle?) In transmedia narrative, a symptomatic example is represented by the *McGuffin*, typical of Hitchcock's narratives, echoed across media, in order to involve the audiences of the given narrative more intimately.

2. *The Unconscious Wound*: a weak point or shadowy area the protagonist is not aware of, inside him or herself, and must now inevitably deal with. In transmedia narratives this issue is generally not explicitly revealed, with its presence left to the audience's deduction, or it can be evoked in a more advanced stage of the narrative, as a part of the live imagery of the story.

3. *Inciting Incident*: also called the *catalyst*. The part of the story in which the Protagonist encounters the problem that will profoundly change his life. The different media involved in the narrative have the ability to show it from different viewpoints, leading the audience to choose which side to be on.

4. *Objective*: according to his or her objective, the protagonist of a given narrative attempts (comically, adventurously or dramatically) to overcome his or her ghost and, without knowing it, heal his or her unconscious wound. It is quite common that, in transmedia narratives, the protagonist's objective is combined with those specific to the audience such as victory points, rewarding powers or visibility within the narrative communities of the tale.

5. *Antagonist*: a character pursuing the same aim as the hero's, only with different motivations, though coherent and reliable. The antagonist is the bearer of completely different ideals than those of the hero; in a transmedia narrative the extent and nature of space given to the antagonist within a given media must always be clear from the initial planning phase, more so in competitive communication systems.

6. *The War*: rather than the actual conflict between hero and antagonist, this is the preparation for the final confrontation between their own worlds, their own ways of interpreting life and death, their own personal universes. In transmedia narratives this is the moment of leaving the "microphones open" and let the audiences confront each other, without fear of *flamers* or excessively trying to manipulate the debate.

7. *Facing Death*: the final duel with the antagonist is preceded by an intimate confrontation between the hero and his or her self. The hero pays Death a visit to which he or she will act in a way that will lead him or her to redemption, or to an irretrievable defeat. In transmedia narrative this is the only instance when the narrative must go back into the hands of its original author.

8. *Final Battle*: only one of the contestants shall eventually reach the shared goal. In this perspective, in transmedia tales each medium involved must have the possibility of expressing its own viewpoint, according to its own language. This is, moreover, the space which is most devoted to the entertainment dimension, as well as that which provides a reward for the public, for example thanks to events or contests.

9. *Awakening*: at the end of the battle a new viewpoint tells another hero's story. It consists of a new awareness, at times a real *understanding*, as in ancient classical drama. On other occasions there is simply an escape to a new world or a newer immersion into the protagonist's ordinary environment. In this case, each medium is free to tell such a passage in its own way.

10. *Transformation of the double*: during the course of the final battle, the Antagonist goes through a path of mutation and awakening, similar to that undergone by the Protagonist. Of course, as a consequence, the story changes again. An example? Identities exchanged by two families who

do not know each other at the end of a holiday, in the ending of a *swap show*[83].

11.   *New balance*: defeater or defeated, together with their followers, returns to the initial world of the story, even though it is not what it used to be. An important change occurred in their existence and so it will have to be with the audience. In transmedia narratives this is the second and last celebrative occasion where contests or events, both physical and online, can be organized in order to completely integrate the project's audiences and communities. Obviously they do so by recalling the most touching passages of the story.

12.   *Thematic revelation*: subtly, the basic message of the story becomes universal to the public's eyes, remembering that, as already pointed out in the previous chapter, the theme of the narrative (the protagonist's unconscious wound) is more effective if invisible during the whole course of the tale.

Once a story told using the "twelve stations" ends, it is ready to be shared, commented upon and "carried on" by one or "n" authors all over the world, in the same media frame or in others. Forums and archives, for instance, grant a generally higher degree of interactivity to a transmedia narrative, and are therefore more appropriate to synergistic actions by communities and authors spread all over the Net. A personal example?

The creation of my transmedia independent project *Proiettiliperscrittori* (*Bullets for writers*) dates back to 2003. It was the first transmedia project I worked on, and it represented an original case of user-determined narrative[84] in those years.

---

[83] *Swap* are those narratives and formats (for reality, game, show and fiction) where the story provides for a planned exchange of role or frame, among the protagonists of the narrative, but not of identity.
[84] About the definition of 'user-determined narrative' P. Sermon, *The emergence of user- and performer-determined narratives in telematic environments*, in: A. Zapp (ed.) *Networked Narrative Environments: As Imaginary Spaces of Being* (2004).

Originally planned as a creative writing lab, initially spread through radio and web TV, its *competitive system* was supported by a blog and a novel to be strongly influenced by the audience. In its radio incarnation, for instance, *Proiettiliperscrittori* was a show made of twelve episodes of advice on writing broadcast by a speaker and combined with examples taken from cinema and television narratives. At the end of each show, an expert speaking from home would give his ratings and evaluations via blog and his contribution was submitted to the show's community's own evaluation. The debate would carry on during the following five days, while on the sixth, the one before the next show, a new subject would be launched, with preparatory links, bibliography and filmography shared with the public. The project went as far as to allow the listener to implement the last three radio shows and one was even read by a regular follower. A video version was, in the meantime, available on web TV, linked to the *Proiettiliperscrittori* blog. But the most important change, and its moment of highest degree of interactivity, was reached thanks to the connection to publishing and the printed paper. In the summer of 2004, in fact, right after the end of the radio show, I launched a new format via blog: a textual web fiction divided into episodes called *Fuoco ci vuole* (*Fire, we need*). Following this format, an episode of the series was broadcast online on the blog around midnight every three days. Each episode of *Fuoco ci vuole* was subdivided into two parts, separated by a ten-minute pause in the process of online publishing. Each part was enriched by a photograph or image found on the web or submitted by the readers. Moreover, as had already happened with the radio show, the following day was dedicated to the readers' comments. In the next 24 hours the episode was corrected and reorganized following the suggestions which emerged in the online debate.

Fuoco ci vuole told the story of a clumsy summer experienced by four friends who go through all sorts of adventures in a deserted and hostile Rome. The characters were living, both individually and chorally, four variations of the twelve stations paradigm, and the story was rich with filmic and literary quotes, which were sent to the public in the form of a contest. The hunt for the locations named in the story was frantic, as pictures and comments were coming in a flood and soon represented a further modality of interactive consumption. The public immediately elected its favourite character among the four in the plot and kept following its role in the narrative, contributing with suggestions for plots, relationships, and dialogues (some of which were used, while others were not), always in a perspective of (online) reasoning and confrontation. Supported by a wide community of faithful followers of the whole project, only two weeks after the twenty-sixth and last episode was posted online, *Fuoco ci vuole* was bought by a publisher and went through a further "re-mediation": initially conceived as a radio screenplay, it later transformed into a web fiction, and in the spring of 2005 became the first transmedia novel ever published in Italy. Thanks to its audience. Together with its audience.

CHAPTER SIX

Different Approaches

As you get closer to the end of a journey, you inevitably start feeling lonely. We all do. We all tend to consider our perspective *the* perspective, and the most reasonable, if not the only possible. We look back and all the memories we have collected seem to be so many, too many, and so vivid as to be able to tell the story themselves. This is the reason why I asked some friends of mine, researchers, editors and producers whose professionalism is acknowledged worldwide, to collaborate to the writing of this final chapter by giving me a short contribution on their own personal approach to transmedia storytelling. I have asked them four questions each, and you will find their answer in the following pages. I sincerely hope they will re-create, thanks to their different perspectives, integrative and complementary viewpoints to those I have expressed in this book. The question asked were:

- Your personal idea of transmedia storytelling asks audiences to…
- Your personal idea of transmedia storytelling drives authors to…

- When you look for the best idea for a transmedia project, you start thinking to…
- The power of Transmedia Storytelling to tell "inner stories" through different media consists in…

And to your own facility they have been duplicated before each answer in each contribution.

Drew Davidson

Drew Davidson is a professor, producer and player of interactive media. His background spans academic, industry and professional worlds and he is interested in stories across texts, comics, games and other media. He is the Director of the Entertainment Technology Center – Pittsburgh at Carnegie Mellon University.

1) Your personal idea of transmedia storytelling asks audiences to…

Transmedia storytelling invites audiences to become a part of a fictional world. It's more than just getting more interactively involved with a narrative, it's about getting immersed in a fictional world and feeling like you have agency within that world, that what you do matters and has an impact on the related story you experiences as you travel across and between media to participate more fully in the story.

2) Your personal idea of transmedia storytelling drives authors to…

Transmedia storytelling enables authors to share their fictional worlds with their audiences and to create emergent experiences that have the potential to evolve in conjunction with their audiences input and participation. Authors help create the canon of the fictional world and can work with their audiences to develop various narratives within the world as characters, events and stories interweave throughout the world.

3) When you look for the best idea for a transmedia project, you start thinking to…

With a transmedia project, you start thinking of the fictional world and how you can create an experience that can have multiple points of entry to encourage a diversity of audience members to get engaged. One of the more successful design strategies is to consider a major tent pole media experience that can support these multiple transmedia rabbit holes into the fictional worlds.

4) The power of Transmedia Storytelling to tell "inner stories" through different media consists in…

The power of transmedia storytelling is to enable us, as audience members to experience our own stories within a fictional world. We can do this on our own, and we can do this together. In both cases, we have the opportunity to engage within a world and feel that our participation has an impact on the events within the overarching narrative.

Christy Dena

Christy Dena is Director of Universe Creation 101 where she develops her own projects, works as an experience designer and writer on transmedia projects, and consults on the expansion of films, TV shows, alternate reality games and performance projects around the world. Recent finished projects she has worked on include Cisco's The Hunt with No

Mimes Media; Tim Kring, The company P & Nokia's Emmy-nominated Conspiracy for Good; and ABC's Project Bluebird. Christy co-wrote the Australian Literature Board's Writer's Guide to Making a Digital Living, wrote the first PhD on Transmedia Practice, and curated Transmedia Victoria. *She began her career as a performer and writer of comedy cabaret, and producer and director of multimedia theatre. She was a digital effects producer for Australian's first fully-digital production studio, working on TVCs, websites and CD-Roms. Christy is a speaker worldwide who has given presentations for TEDxTransmedia; Whistler Film Festival; Cartoons on the Bay; Power to the Pixel; and many more.*

1) Your personal idea of transmedia storytelling asks audiences to…

Transmedia projects appear to ask audiences to be more active with the worlds they experience. For instance, "the audience" has to move from watching television to visiting a website, or from reading a graphic novel to watching a movie in a theatre, or from speaking to someone on a phone to running through the streets on a mission. But these are things people do everyday anyway. The difference with transmedia is that they now do these things to experience the same fictional (or factual) world. It requires perceiving a world in all its guises, engaging with many artforms, and seeing them all as being part of some greater whole. Transmedia can at times even ask audiences to speak to characters, suggest sub-plots, create new assets, and be the protagonist. Transmedia often asks of audiences what they've been doing anyway! You could say they just haven't been able to be themselves with entertainment before.

2) Your personal idea of transmedia storytelling drives authors to…

Transmedia drives authors to think episodically. There is no great conclusion at the end of a medium, it is more of a corner. It asks authors to view all artforms as equal. One isn't a primary medium and another tertiary to be used purely for distribution or promotion. Instead, each medium can be a part of the meaning-making process. It asks authors to be collaborative and multi-lingual. They need to communicate and work with people from a range of siloed artforms and industries each with their own jargon, values and production processes. Transmedia asks authors gather all that they love into their arms and figure out how to make them work together. They need to be skilled at many trades, and a master at combining them.

3) When you look for the best idea for a transmedia project, you start thinking to...

Putting aside what I personally find interesting in terms of subject matter, a transmedia project needs certain elements to work. Usually it needs to be episodic in nature. Not all writers are aware of this. I have been sent many film scripts that are obviously written for a single experience: the film. The writer is not trained in TV or web, or book serials at all and so thinks in terms of the single story. What this means is there is often nothing substantial enough to explore further elsewhere. The film is full of endings. It is complete in itself. Depending on the transmedia form, it may also needs to facilitate interaction. Is it a world where players can have a role in it in some way? Is it something people want to spend time in, and is there a good enough reason to be active in it? And in some cases, does it permit the inclusion of the player's actual world too? Ultimately too, does it cry out for a multi-artform expression? Is it bursting at the seams and deserve to be in more places than one? Does it need a live event and broadcast element, for instance, or a musty book and knitting game?

4) The power of Transmedia Narrative to tell "inside stories" is...

The majority of good stories take the characters through a journey. To me, I find both external and internal obstacles interesting. The multi-form nature of transmedia lends itself to providing different perspectives. This means we can venture much further into a character, and their relationships with others. In one medium we find the characters going through a narrative arc, but then we can also delve further and discover a previous narrative arc that makes their recent one even more significant. This is one of the beautiful aspects of transmedia: the cumulative effect of depth across time and space. And of course, given that transmedia requires an audience to actively join the dots across media and also play a role in the storyworld, the whole experience can facilitate a player journey too. As players spend time with characters, they potentially grow with them.

Jeff Gomez

Jeff Gomez is CEO *of Starlight Runner Entertainment and has worked on such blockbuster universes as Disney's* Pirates of the Caribbean, Prince of Persia *and* Tron, *for brands like Coca Cola and Mattel, and for franchises as* Avatar *and* Transformers. *He is one of the most important transmedia producers in the world.*

1) Your personal idea of transmedia storytelling asks audiences to...

The best transmedia storytelling experiences invite audience members to immerse themselves in the story world, exploring different aspects of character and incident, journeying to "distant mountains" which are aspects of the story world that may not be obvious but are worth finding. The best of these experiences also invite audience members to somehow contribute to the dialog that is the best of what storytelling communication holds. A truly interactive transmedia experience is signified by the participant's ability not simply to choose between two threats of narrative but to impact the narrative itself.

2) Your personal idea of transmedia storytelling drives authors to…

The best transmedia storytelling experiences drives authors to consider the audience members' engagement with the narrative, particularly as it is mediated through various technologies. How is the story told differently through the mobile platform than it is as a graphic novel? How does the story play to the strengths of the video game platform? And because we live in an age where the very media that delivers the story can be used by the participant to invite more people to the experience (or tell them to stay away), authors must make an extra effort to enrich and refine the story itself. Quality is the winner of the Digital Age.

3) When you look for the best idea for a transmedia project, you start thinking to…

Rich, fully realized story worlds provide the best possible foundation for a transmedia project. Creators must start with a superb story, supported by compelling and identifiable characters, but then extra work must go into developing a highly detailed and sustainable world, a "world worthy of devotion".

4) The power of Transmedia Storytelling to tell "inner stories" through different media consists in…

"Inner stories" signify the power of intimacy that some media are now capable of engendering. Web and mobile platforms, which are highly individualized and intimate, are especially adept at conveying the psychology and emotion of a story that would otherwise be epic in proportion as a movie or video game. Of course, we can't forget the novel as a medium perfectly suited to convey the "inner story" of characters we are growing to love.

Lance Weiler

Lance Weiler is a story architect of film, tv, games and storyworlds. Considered to be a thought leader in the space, Lance sits on a World Economic Forum steering committee for the future of content creation and teaches participatory storytelling at Columbia University. "Wired" magazine named him "One of twenty-five people helping to re-invent entertainment and change the face of Hollywood" due to the way he makes and distributes his work. In 2006 Lance created the WorkBook Project *as an open creative network for storytellers and in 2008 he a co-founded* DIY DAYS *a roving conference for those who create. Lance is currently developing a slate projects that are positioned well for storytelling in the 21st century.*

1)   Your personal idea of transmedia storytelling asks audiences to...

Audience is dead. The reality is that what was once an audience is now what I consider to be collaborators. The relationship has totally changed. Democratization of tools turns audiences into their own media companies free to push button publish for the world to see. Authorship is shifting and as a result more people can be part of the storytelling. So in that sense participatory storytelling is an opportunity to take advantage of the connected world we currently live in. For me personally transmedia asks people to collaborate and to co-create stories that can be jumping off points to social connections and if I do that the stories will surely spread.

2) Your personal idea of transmedia storytelling drives authors to...

To experiment. I feel that we are in a period of story research and development. That by spending time expanding the ways in which we tell stories we are bound to discover new ways for people to connect. We will also come across new business models to sustain not only for the authors but also those who contribute within the storyworlds that we create. The challenge is for storytellers to stop and listen and realize that it is actually about a conversation.

3) Thinking to the best idea for a transmedia project in your opinion, you would start mentioning...

My process embraces elements of design thinking, game development, storytelling and business development. Over time I've built an organic process that helps me to develop the storyworlds I wish to share. Transmedia if not more than traditional forms of storytelling needs time to develop. Since there are so many possibilities it is important to take the time to live with elements of what you hope the storyworld will include. For instance we will experiment and do so often. We will look to fail quickly and learn from those mistakes. It is an ongoing process. Take it to where the people are. Let them touch it, let them break it. Learn from that and continue to revise and develop. So in the end it is about giving the work time to grow.

4)   The powerful strenght of Transmedia Storytelling to tell "inside stories" (of characters or of particular universes) on different media consists in...

I challenge a lot of what is defined as transmedia. To me it is about a narrative flow. It could be a single screen with real world elements or it could be three or more screens. Don't let the definitions or the desire to have a simple solution lock you down. This is an amazing time for storytellers as the art of story is evolving. Don't mistake it as a revolution because the way forward embraces the learnings of the past but must recognize that much of the technology and infrastructure to tell transmedia stories effectively doesn't exist. Too much of an effort is placed on the audience. The barrier to entry is often to great. It is important to challenge ourselves to find the core of the story and the themes we wish to mine. From there the we can identify the path for the narrative flow. For the best ways for the characters to move across a particular universe.

EPILOGUE

It was July 2004 when the news that Microsoft had registered "the human body as an apparatus able to transmit electric current and data" with the American Patent and Trademark Office quickly spread its echo all over the world, evoking on the international press scenarios typical of science fiction (some media recalled the identity between medium and user of *precogs* in *Minority Report*, while some others mentioned the machine synthesizing connective intelligence in *Strange Days*). The corporate promptly explained that *only* the skin was to be considered object of such an operation – being an excellent conductor – as to connect the different devices which, in the future, could be plugged into the human body: mobile phones, music and video players…

The most frequent question in those days was if that was eventually to be the ultimate way the media would find to inhabit us- to crossbreed and interbreed with our imagery and emotions. Apart from all the possible provocations, a few years on and with platforms refreshing themselves on a monthly basis, the media we can count on today still fulfil sufficiently their tasks, and the actual digital revolution evoked around the world will be made on the territory of content and of the form, on their fruition.

The *genetic mutation of language* parallel to such a process is another factor leading new authors of contemporary narratives into being more and more transmedial. Hopefully, soon, also the spaces and the scenarios where to practically use the narrative techniques investigated in these pages shall widen up to include new territories of action: from scientific research to cultural integration, from socially responsible activities to global knowledge re-distribution.

If the dream of a transmedia cooperation between world audiences still appears to be some sort of utopia, it is also a fact that within the meshes of the Net, some projects are starting to raise their voice, aiming at reducing the world gap in accessing the planet's resources or at enhancing social, economical and political integration of minorities, and the developing countries. On the one hand the technological conditions. So, the goal to be reached as for today is to make – day after day – the *mediasphere* a less violent and improvised territory, more able to reach the single user and interact with him or her. A place rich with respect and good stories, open and truly transmedia, not much to be depicted as a net and more similar to the breathable atmosphere of a planet. Or to its pollen. And this both in the case of transmedia achieving a more careful, selecting and moderate penetration in the next future, and in the case of it flooding the planet ahead like the unstoppable tsunami.

This is the reason why the hypothesis and the message with which I'm closing our journey and this book go even beyond the famous Microsoft patent. Hypothesis and message which tend to consider the human mind (both in its emotional and rational sides) as the real transmedia interface of the future, they consign into the hand of transmedia storytelling the ambitious challenge of learning to tell new stories for a better future, thus creating a new Esperanto, a new return to orality.

The mythopoesis of tomorrow's narratives already is going beyond the distance exiting between perception and image Sartre was talking about, and, when this will come about, as Henry Jenkins following Marshall McLuhan's researches is pointing out, it will happen without the abolition of neither the narrative's primordial canons nor the necessity for media. During the course of human history, in fact, it was the instruments to access content, which died out, not the means of communication. The latter get replaced, while the former evolve[85].

We will therefore need to keep our eyes wide open for the emergence of new narrative forms. Let us prick up our ears on today's metamorphosis of storytelling and narrative subverters, authors, users, fan and early adopters who do not give up the idea of contaminating or violating entertainment's and narrative sacred brands, with the aim of using multiplatform media in order to show us new modalities of self-representation and renewal of collective imagery. As the new "trilobites of narratives" living in techno-dramaturgical habitats of the future, they will be as a matter of fact the new owners of the "machine of dreams". Them, the new bards, pioneers of the next frontiers of transmedia storytelling.

---

[85] H. Jenkins, *Convergence…* cit. (2006).

BIBLIOGRAPHY

BOOKS

Abruzzese, A., Ragone, G. (eds.), *Letteratura fluida*, Liguori Editore, Napoli 2007.

Adorno T. *The Culture Industry, selected essays on mass culture*, Introduzione di J. M. Bernstein, Routledge, London-New York 1991.

Anderson, B., *Comunità immaginate. Origine e diffusione dei nazionalismi*, ManifestoLibri, Roma 1996.

Anderson, C., '*Disneyland*', in: Newcomb, H. (a cura di), *Television. The Critical View*, Oxford University Press, New York 1994.

Bachtin, M., *Epos e romanzo*, in: Janovič, C. S. (a cura di), *Estetica e romanzo*, Einaudi, Torino 1979.

Barthes, R., *La morte dell'autore*, in: *Il brusio della lingua*, Einaudi, Torino 1980.

Baudrillard, J., *Il sistema degli oggetti*, Bompiani, Milano 2006.

Bekenstein, J., *Buchi neri, comunicazione, energia*, Di Renzo Editore, Roma 2001.

Biressi, A., *Reality TV: realism and revelation*, Wallflower Press, London 2005.

Bolter, J. D., Grusin, R. *Remediation. Competizione e integrazione tra media vecchi e nuovi*, Angelo Guerini Editore, Milano 2003.

Branswyn, G., *Jamming the media: a citizen's guide: reclaiming the tools of communication*, Chronicle Books, San Francisco 1997.

Broker, W., *Using the Force: Creativity, Community and Star Wars Fans*, Continuum, New York 2002.

Calvino, I., *Lezioni Americane. Sei proposte per il prossimo millennio*, Mondadori, Milano 1998.

Campbell, J., *The Hero with a Thousand Faces*, Princeton University Press, Princeton 1968

Castells, M., *The Internet Galaxy: Reflections on the Internet, Business and Society*, Oxford University Press, Oxford 2001.

de Certeau, M., *L'invenzione del quotidiano*, Edizioni Lavoro, Roma 2001.

De Kerckhove, D., *Brainframes. Mente, Tecnologia. Mercato*, Baskerville, Bologna 1993.

Dancyger, K., Rush, J., *Alternative scriptwriting*, Focal Press, Boston 1991.

Davies, P., *Gli ultimi tre minuti. Congetture sul destino dell'universo*, Sansoni, Milano 1995.

Debord, G., *La società dello spettacolo*, Baldini e Castoldi, Milano 1967.

Doctorow, C., *Down and Out in the Magic Kingdom*, TOR Books, New York 2003.

Donaton, S., *Madison and Wine: Why the Entertainment and Advertising Industries Must Converge to Survive*, McGraw-Hill, New York 2004.

Durand, G., *Les Structures anthropologiques de l'imaginaire*, Allie, Grenoble 1960.

Eco, U., *Lector in fabula*, Bompiani, Milano 1979.

Fiedler, L., *The Middle Against Both Ends*, in: *The Collected Essays*, Vol. II, Stein & Day, New York 1971.

Field, S., *La sceneggiatura*, Lupetti Editore, Milano 1997.

Flew, T., *New Media: an introduction*, Oxford University Press, South Melbourne (2008)

Flowers, B. S., *Joseph Campbell's The Power of Myth with Bill Moyers*, Anchor Books, New York 1988.

Forlai, L., Bruni, A., *Come raccontare una grande storia che appassioni il pubblico*, Dino Audino Editore, Roma 1996.

Frazer Lamb, P., Veith, D., *Romantic Myth, Trascendence, and Star Trek Zines*, in: Palumbo, D. (a cura di), *Erotic Universe: Sexuality and Fantastic Literature*, Greenwood Press, New York 1986, pp. 235-256.

Freeland, C., *Ordinary Horror on Reality TV*, in: Freeland, C., *Narrative across Media: The Languages of Storytelling*, University of Nebraska Press, Lincoln 2004.

Gee, P. J., *Semiotic Social Spaces and Affinity Spaces: From The Age of Mythology to Today's Schools*, in: D. Barton, K. Tusting (Eds.), *Beyond communities of practice: Language, power and social context*, Cambridge University Press, Cambridge 2005, pp. 214-232.

Genette, G., *Soglie. I dintorni del testo*, Einaudi, Torino 1989.

Giovagnoli, M., *All'immobilità qualcosa sfugge*, MeridianoZero, Padova 2008.

     – *Cross-media. Le nuove narrazioni*, Apogeo, Milano 2009.

     – *Fare cross-media. Dal Grande Fratello a Star Wars. Teoria e tecniche della comunicazione integrata e distribuita nei media*, Dino Audino Editore, Roma 2005.

Gobe, M., *Emotional Branding: The New Paradigm for Connecting Brands to People*, Allworth Press, New York 2001.

Godin, S., *Permission Marketing. Turning Strangers into Friends, and Friends into Customers*, Simon & Schuster, New York 1999.

Greimas, A. J., *Del senso 2. Narratività, Modalità, Passioni*, Bompiani, Milano 1984.

     – *La semantica strutturale: ricerca di metodo*, Rizzoli, Milano 1968.

Haas Dyson, A., *Writing Superheroes: Contemporary Childhood, Popular Culture, and Classroom Literacy*, Teachers College Press, New York 1997.

Hills, M., *Fan Cultures*, Routledge, London 2002.

Jenkins, H., *Cultura convergente*, Apogeo, Milano 2007.

     – *Fans, Gamers and Bloggers*, New York University Press, New York 2003.

     – *Textual Poachers: Television Fans and Participatory Culture*, Routledge, New York 1991.

Jung, C.G., *Gli archetipi dell'inconscio collettivo*, Einaudi, Torino 1968.

Kosinetz, R.V., *E-Tribalized Marketing? The Strategic Implications of Virtual Communities of Consumption*, in "European Managment Journal", 17/3/1999, pp. 252-264.

Laurel, B., *Design Research: Methods and Perspectives*, MIT Press, Cambridge, Mass. 2004.

Lévy, P., *Collective Intelligence: Mankind's Emerging World in Cyberspace*, Perseus Books, Cambridge, Mass. 1997.

Lotman, J. M., *La Semiosfera*, Marsilio Editore, Venezia 1985.

Marks, D., *Inside Story. The Power of the Transformational Arc*, Three Mountains Press, Los Angeles 2007.

Marshall, D,. *The New Intertextual Commodity*, in: Harris, D. (a cura di), *The Book of New Media*, British Film Institute, London 2002, pp. 69-81.

McGracken, G., *Produzione del significato e del movimento nel mondo dei beni*, in: Di Nallo, E. (a cura di), *Il significato sociale del consumo*, Laterza, Roma-Bari 1999.

McLuhan, M., *Gli strumenti del comunicare*, Milano 1967.

Morcellini, M., *Il mediaevo. Tv e industria culturale nell'Italia del XX secolo*, Carocci Editore, Roma 2000.

Morin, E., *L'industria culturale*, il Mulino, Bologna 1963, Bantam Books, New York 1979.

Negroponte, N., *Being Digital*, Alfred A. Knopf, New York 1995.

Palumbo, D. (Ed.) *Erotic Universe: Sexuality and Fantastic Literature*, Greenwood, New York 1986.

Pecchinenda, G., *Videogiochi e cultura della simulazione. La nascita dell'«homo game»*, Laterza, Bari 2003.

Propp, V. J., *Morphology of the Folktale*, University of Texas Press, Austin 1968.

Rifkin, J., *L'era dell'accesso*, Mondadori, Milano 1997.

Rheingold, H., *Smart Mobs: The Next Social Revolution*, Basic Books, New York 2002.

Roberts, K., *Lovemarks: The Future Beyond Brand*, Power House Books, New York 2004.

Sartre, Jean-Paul, *L'Imaginaire: Psychologie phénoménologique de l'imagination*, Gallimard, Paris 1940.

Searle, J., *The Literary Enneagram. Characters from Inside Out*, Metamorphous Press, Portland 2001.

Sermon, P., *The emergence of user- and performer-determined narratives in telematic environments*, in: A. Zapp (ed.) *Networked Narrative Environments: As Imaginary Spaces of Being* Manchester Metropolitan University, Manchester 2004, pp. 82-98.

Siegel, D., *Pull : The Power of the Semantic Web to Transform Your Business*, Portfolio, New York 2009.

Truffaut, F., *Le cinéma selon Hitchcock*, Robert Laffont, Paris 1967.

Uricchio, W., Pearson, R. E., (eds), *The Many Lives of the Batman: Critical Approaches to a Superhero and His Media*, Routledge, New York 1991.

Ventriglia, G., *Sulle drammaturgie non lineari*, in: "Script", 30/31, 2002, pp. 41-46.

Vogler, C., *The Writer's Journey*, Michael Wiese Productions, Los Angeles 2007.

Wheeler, J. A., Rees, M., *Black Holes, Gravitational Waves, and Cosmology*, Gordon and Breach, New York 1974.

WEBSITES AND ONLINE RESOURCES

http://blog.thoughtpick.com/
http://campfirenyc.com/
http://festival.machinima.org/
http://machinima.com
http://narrware.com/
http://starlightrunner.com/
http://starwars.com/eu/
http://tedxtransmedia.com/2011/
http://thepenguinblog.typepad.com/the_penguin_blog/2007/03/a_million_pengu.html
http://vforvendetta.warnerbros.com/
http://waxebb.com/
http://wwjbmovie.com/
http://www.archive.nu
http://www.christydena.com/
http://www.efpfanfic.net/
http://www.googlelittrips.org/
http://www.henryjenkins.org/
http://www.ibelieveinharleydent.com
http://www.ibelieveinharveydenttoo.com
http://www.kpe.com
http://www.lucasfilm.com/divisions/
http://www.myspace.com/paulocoelho
http://www.myspace.com/quarterlife
http://www.syfy.com/
http://www.siemens.it/buildygame
http://www.starwreck.com/
http://www.subvertising.org
http://www.thesecret.tv
http://www.youtube.com/watch?v=YNH2AXBxcsQ
http://www.webserials.com
http://www.whysoserious.com
http://www.wired.com/wired/archive/12.10/tail_pr.html